PEAK
PUBS
A PINT-SIZED HISTORY

Andrew McCloy

HALSGROVE

First published by Halsgrove in 2005

Cover photograph: *The Devonshire Arms at Pilsley*

British Library Cataloguing-in-Publication Data.
A CIP record for this title is available from the British Library.

ISBN 1 84114 450 9

HALSGROVE
Halsgrove House
Lower Moor Way
Tiverton EX16 6SS
T: 01884 243242
F: 01884 243325
www.halsgrove.com

Printed and bound in Great Britain by
The Cromwell Press, Trowbridge

Contents

Acknowledgments

Thanks to Jim McIntosh, from the Campaign for Real Ale (Chesterfield and District branch), for his advice and information, especially regarding the Derby Tup. I'm also indebted to the Dore Village Society for permission to reproduce details about the Old Horse, and to a number of other local heritage groups who have produced some fascinating and valuable research. These include the Hathersage Millennium Group, Elton Local History Group, Bakewell & District Historical Society, Winster Local History Group, Bonsall History Project, Hope Historical Society and Eyam Village Society. Also, grateful thanks to Roly Smith, David Allingham, Tony Wilkin and Nicky Crewe, Sean and Jo Healey, as well as Julie Bunting and the Peakland Heritage Project for allowing me to dip into www.peaklandheritage.org, an excellent resource run by Derbyshire County Council's Libraries and Heritage Department.

Introduction:
Mine's a Pint

"Nay, I am for the country liquor, Derbyshire ale, if you please; for a man should not, methinks, come up from London to drink wine in the Peak." So said Dr Johnson, the famous eighteenth-century lexicographer and raconteur, and a man who clearly visited plenty of inns and taverns on his travels.

If he were alive today it would be fascinating to hear his opinions on how the pubs of the Peak District have changed; but some of them we can probably guess at. I imagine he would be uneasy at the creeping commercialism that is turning some pubs into characterless restaurants; at the blandness and predictability of many pub menus; and how relentless piped music subdues what, for Dr Johnson, was a key ingredient of the public house – good conversation. I suspect he wouldn't exactly rave about Alcopops or cold gassy lager, either, although it must be said that there were some decidedly odd concoctions served up in his day.

However, there are still plenty of pubs and inns dotted around the Peak District where he almost certainly would feel at home, and where I can picture him sitting by the fireside or perched on a stool (or two) by the bar and holding forth on the issues of the day. Once he had got over paying over two pounds for a pint of best bitter, I can see him settling down and entertaining the assembled audience with one anecdote after another, and creating that timeless bonhomie that comes with a relaxed, social drink and a darn good chat.

Mind you, just like the alehouses, town taverns and coaching inns of Dr Johnson's time, the present-day pubs of the Peak District are a mixed bag, and reflect what is a diverse and endlessly fascinating region. In this book I'm treating the Peak District in the widest sense – from the Staffordshire Moorlands to the South Yorkshire Pennines; from the Derwent valley in the east to the Cheshire hills out to the west – and beyond the artificial confines of the Peak District National Park.

The pubs range from isolated moorland cottages to bustling town centre bars, former coaching inns to historic hotels; although for a region that is overwhelmingly rural in nature, the traditional village inn remains the cornerstone of this study. We look back at over three centuries of social upheaval through the eyes of the public house: farming, mining, industry, tourism – all of these are reflected in the fortunes of the 'local'.

And what stories some of them can tell. Most of these tales are true, or at least started off rooted in fact; some of them were probably a little iffy to begin with and were no doubt embroidered through repeated telling; and a small number were almost certainly rubbish from the outset, but are so entertaining that I have relayed them anyway (with a clear health warning).

Many of these stories have emanated, quite properly, from the pubs, publicans and pub-goers themselves, and to all of them I am extremely grateful. It has been a truly wonderful book to write. Who else can say that they're just popping down the pub for "a spot of research"?

However, I have also spent time delving among a wealth of fascinating and worthy local publications compiled by the likes of local historians and village heritage groups, many of which have provided priceless first-hand information, and the key ones are listed in the bibliography. The best way to record which pubs once stood where and what they were like is to speak to those people who once drank in them, and through this we can also add to the overall history of our local communities.

The Great British pub

As with so many other aspects of everyday life that we now take for granted, the origin of the Great British Pub can be traced back to the Romans. It was their thirsty footsloggers who needed regular refreshment stops, and this led to the emergence of the first alehouses. As the saying goes, fermentation and civilisation went hand in hand.

By medieval times, drinking establishments had become a permanent fixture in settlements across the country; but foreshadowing more recent concerns about the effects of so-called binge drinking, the authorities made attempts to curb the number of alehouses in any one village, as well as the amount that an individual could drink. Around AD 970 pegs were introduced to the inside of wooden drinking cups to indicate the maximum amount that each person could drink before handing it on to someone else – hence the common expression 'taking a person down a peg or two'.

Early inns provided accommodation for weary travellers – from pilgrims to soldiers and merchants – and as transport and communications developed so did the range and number of licensed premises that offered hospitality, as well as a place of refuge from the toil and hardships of everyday life.

Pubs have played a central role in our society ever since, and whether your fascination is with names and signboards, architecture and design, or simply the enjoyment of a good pint of beer, there is nearly always something of interest to be found in an authentic and well-run public house.

Free beer tomorrow

The uniqueness of the British pub has struck me hardest when I've been abroad for long periods. Only then do I look back and think how peculiar it seems to simply walk into what in effect is someone else's home and ask for a drink. And some of the more personalised and intimate public houses really do feel like someone else's private front room. For me, this book has revealed the incredible diversity of pubs in the Peak District, and that so much is down to the personality of the individual publican.

As much as people might view their traditional local as their own private and cosy little world, pubs are inevitably businesses, and I've been surprised and a little dismayed at how many pubs I've visited recently that have 'For Sale' or 'Pub to Let' signs in the windows. It's inevitable that some establishments will go under – and you only have to look at the long list of ex-pubs in Chapter 8 to see what has gone before – but the rate that country pubs, in particular, are closing is alarming.

I hope that this book will encourage you to seek out some of the more unusual and interesting pubs and inns of the Peak District, and by doing so I hope it will help these places survive and even prosper. They certainly deserve to, for bound up in these wonderful places is a heritage that is as rich and potent as the stuff that comes foaming out of the pumps at the bar.

Once more, I find myself returning to the wise words of Dr. Johnson: "No, Sir, there is nothing which has yet been contrived by man, by which so much happiness is produced as by a good tavern or inn." I'll drink to that!

2
A Traditional Way of Life

The age of the alehouse

It may come as something of a surprise to learn that the quaint picture of the traditional village pub or country inn is relatively new, with most dating from the 1700s.

Of course, there are a number of pubs that proudly display notices declaring that their particular establishment dates back much further – oh, till medieval times, at least. Perhaps part of the actual building does; or maybe the present pub replaced a much older dwelling. The Bull i' th' Thorn, on the A515 south east of Buxton, claims to date from 1472, replacing an original twelfth century farmstead. The Olde Bulls Head at Little Hucklow, off the Bradwell-Tideswell road, also boasts a lineage going back to the twelfth-century, and asserts that it is the fifth oldest pub in England.

In early medieval times, households tended to brew their own alcohol, and communal brewing was also common. The surplus would often be sold on to neighbours or anyone else that happened to be passing, and so, with no restrictions on its sale, alehouses became widespread. It was quite common for any reasonably large dwelling to incorporate a so-called brewhouse, and since women often used to undertake the work they were known as alewives.

At some point there must have been a gradual separation between the private house, where ale was dispensed directly out of the dwelling, and what were clearly commercial premises which expressly catered for those who wanted to stop for a drink and perhaps a bed for the night. It was out of the latter, of course, that what we understand today as the public house or inn emerged.

Ultimately it was changing demand and shifts in social behaviour, as well as tighter regulations, that led to the demise of the alehouse. A typical example is the White Peak village of Winster, which once had over 20 alehouses and inns, and where the village stores is even known as the Old Brewhouse. Today just two pubs remain. Eyam, another ex-mining village, is said to have sported as many as 23 alehouses (as well as 11 inns) in the early nineteenth century. In 2005 just the one pub remains.

Back then, ale and beer were different drinks. Ale was originally brewed from water, malt and yeast, and was a popular, everyday drink. It was sweet and not as strong as most beers today, and was probably often safer than local water, since it was effectively sterilised in the brewing process. In 1820, a doctor at Great Longstone, correctly guessing that infected water was responsible for a local epidemic, actually prescribed new beer for the villagers to drink.

'Beer', as we know it today, only came along with the introduction of hops in the late Middle Ages, but since then the two terms have become interchangeable. However, ale and beer ale were such common drinks that they were consumed throughout the day, and bearing in mind this was a time pre-dating morning tea and coffee, there was even a weak brew drunk at breakfast known as 'small beer'(hence the saying: 'Only small beer').

Love it or loathe it, there is no doubting the central role that ale or beer has played in our social development over the centuries. Even the Church embraced brewing, and many religious establishments had brewhouses attached to their premises.

What were known as Church Ales and Whitsun Ales were an annual fixture in the calendar for many communities, including those of the Peak District. It was basically seen as a means for the church to raise extra revenue, as well as an excuse for people to eat and drink to excess, and involved churchwardens collecting malt from all the parishioners in order to brew beer for the whole village. The special brew was presented at a ceremony officiated by a chosen 'lord and lady of the ale', and from all accounts was an excuse for much merry-making. In addition, there were so-called Bid Ales or Help Ales, when villagers got together over a communal brew to raise funds for someone or something specific.

Hospitality for visitors

Pubs, inns and taverns have, from the earliest days, provided hospitality for those visiting or passing through. From monks and merchants through to soldiers and salesmen, the roadside inn has offered refreshment and accommodation for many centuries. Some of the first travellers were pilgrims and religious types, who journeyed between ecclesiastical houses, or from abbeys to outlying granges (farms owned and run by monasteries, sometimes a long distance away).

From Norman times monasteries themselves provided basic hospitality – the hospice – for any passing traveller, including pilgrims en route to the shrines of various saints at home and abroad. Monasteries often brewed their own beer and ale, which would then be dispensed to weary travellers. Indeed, it was accepted that monasteries and religious houses had a duty to offer overnight accommodation to anyone that asked for it; and in some ways, early alehouses did much the same.

As we will also see in the later chapter on the origin of pub names, religion and pubs are (perhaps surprisingly) closely connected. Should you venture a little outside our patch, to Nottingham, be sure to visit Ye Olde Trip to Jerusalem, an historic inn located under the walls of the city's castle. The back bar has even been carved out of the sandstone bedrock underpinning the fortification. The inn claims to be the oldest pub in England, supposedly established around AD 1189 by a group of soldiers preparing for Richard the Lionheart's Crusade to the Holy Lands. However, there is no firm evidence that this is the case, and it is more likely that it was simply a brewhouse established in the 1600s-1700s to serve the castle. Still, it feels very old, and brewers Hardys and Hansons have even named a beer after the pub, so let's go with the story.

Even as late as the 1700s, soldiers were lodged in pubs and inns, since barracks were in fact quite rare until Victorian times. But following on from the early pilgrims and religious crusaders, it was mainly traders and itinerant salesmen who trod the paths and roads and who required board and lodging, and the names of some Peakland pubs still bear testimony to this early role.

There are two called the Traveller's Rest, one located in the Hope Valley at the Bradwell turning, and the other on a bend of the Buxton-Leek road (A53) near the village of Flash, high up on the wild and inhospitable western moors. The latter, in particular, enjoys a striking position, located near the source of the River Manifold.

If you visit the seventeenth-century inn on a bleak winter's day, with the clouds racing across the sky and the wind howling in your ears, you can begin to imagine why those early travellers struggling across the moors were grateful for such places. It claims to be the third highest pub in England, after the Tan Hill Inn and Cat and Fiddle, and is one of those places where the fire can be lit even in the summer. The pub was originally called the Brown Cow, but a mix-up over new pub signs saw it become the Traveller's Rest by mistake, and the name evidently stuck. It was owned for a long time by the Harpur-Crewe family (see Chapter 4) and was gradually extended and adapted over the years.

Its recent heyday was surely the 1970s when the pub held the

Guinness World Record for having an astonishing 76 separate beer pumps on the bar. For a short but colourful period the pub was hugely popular, no doubt helped by the choice of 42 different brews – and the fact that there were five particularly good-looking barmaids. According to someone who was a regular at the time, it was not unusual to have to queue to get in.

Since that time the pub has had a chequered history, and was even closed completely following a tragedy in the early 1990s when a car full of joy-riders failed to negotiate the tight bend outside the pub and ploughed into the main bar. The pub was subsequently sold and the new owners have renovated the interior, reopening for business in 1997.

Luckily much of the original character has been retained, with a series of small and cosy rooms sporting log fires; but what will almost certainly grab your attention initially will be the bizarre array of bric-a-brac, antiques and curios that adorn every nook and cranny. Amassed by the landlord, an inveterate collector, they include antique clocks, musical instruments, hats, old telephones and tea urns, cash registers, brasses and pots – a veritable Aladdin's Cave.

A pub in Hathersage remembers a specific type of traveller through its name. The Scotsman's Pack, on School Lane at the eastern end of the village, takes its name from the packmen, as travelling drapers were sometimes known, who used to visit from Scotland in the 1500s-1600s with their tweeds and woollens, and who went from village to village and farm to farm selling their wares. Sited on the old road to Sheffield, the original building dates from around 1650.

At the rear of the inn there was an area of common land that was often frequented by gypsies, squatters and sheep thieves (it's hard to imagine the good folk of Hathersage putting up with that now). The pub was initially called the Scotchman's Pack, but the name and building changed in 1913 when new landlord William Simpson added the mock Tudor façade, which was a popular architectural addition at the time.

The Scotsman's Pack would almost certainly have also hosted the familiar packhorse trains which wound their way over the Peakland moors. Lines of horses sometimes 40 or 50 strong would regularly criss-cross the hills with their various cargoes of coal, wool, salt, corn, malt, and so on. What a sight they must have been.

The packhorse trains were led by men known as jaggers, whose name possibly originates from the tough German ponies called jaegers that were often used. Lines of these hardy beasts followed ancient routes through the valleys and hills, and crossed rivers and streams by the familiar narrow bridges which walkers still use today. In terms of pubs, they are remembered by an Old Packhorse Inn at Chapel en le Frith, and Packhorse Inns at Crowdecote, Hayfield, New Mills and Little Longstone, near Bakewell (see Chapter 6).

There are former packhorse routes all over the Peak District, some of them walled green lanes and others simply overgrown paths, and although a few are now metalled roads, there are plenty of reminders of their past use if you look closely at local maps. For instance, away on the eastern fringe of the Peak District a packhorse route led from the Kelstedge Inn across the moors to Two Dales, following a route that is still called Jaggers Lane.

Elsewhere, the trains of horses are closely associated with the Hope and Edale valleys, the narrow east-west corridors in the Dark Peak which culminate in Castleton and the bulky hill of Mam Tor. They have given their name to Jaggers Lane in Hathersage, and Jaggers Clough on the eastern slopes of Kinder Scout, and are identified with pubs like the Old Nag's Head at Grindsbrook Booth, Edale, and the Cheshire Cheese Inn at Hope.

Rather confusingly, there's also the Olde Cheshire Cheese at neighbouring Castleton (and others at Buxton and Longnor), all of which allude to one of the commodities plied by the packhorse teams. The Hope pub, which is a lovely little place tucked away on the Edale road half a mile out of the village, used to house the jaggers who carried salt out of Cheshire and, it is said, paid for their overnight lodgings with this famous regional cheese. Today it's cash or credit card, of course.

Cheese and salt would be carried eastwards from Cheshire, while bales of wool would travel in the opposite direction from Yorkshire. Malt and wood often came north from Derby. However, the packhorse ways were often an extension of far more ancient routes.

These included the Portway across the central limestone plateau, used since before Roman times; and the network of saltways emanating from key salt-producing locations such as Northwich in Cheshire and which had been in use since Saxon times. There were also so-called corpse roads, such as the well-established track from the Edale valley over Hollins Cross to Castleton, used to carry the dead for burial at St Edmund's in Castleton before Edale church was consecrated in 1633.

Up until the mid 1600s travel was slow and arduous, with few decent roads and long journey times, but with the coming of the turnpikes everything changed. Stagecoaches dramatically-cut travelling times and coaching inns began to appear on the main routes, where horses would need changing and passengers refreshing. There are still a number of fine old coaching inns in the Peak District, and in the next chapter we will look in more detail at the transport revolution and its effect on the public house.

Not all of the travellers and men of the road who frequented the local inns and taverns were legitimate users, however, and this is borne out by the name of a pub on the road between Macclesfield and Whaley Bridge (B5470) at Rainow.

The Highwayman is a handsome, whitewashed stone building that dates from around 1600 (when it was known as Patch House), and consists of four small and atmospheric rooms. Until 1949 it was called the Blacksmith's Arms, but its renaming is a reminder of one notorious regular from the past. The highwayman in question was Charles Pym, after whom Pym Chair above Errwood Reservoir is named (there was once a chair-shaped rock here, bearing the carved initials 'PC'). He is said to have used the pub as his hideout as he went about his business of robbing travellers on the surrounding highways.

A place in the country

The village pubs and alehouses of the Peak District have always enjoyed an important role in community life, and for a variety of reasons. As we will see in the next chapter, lead mining was once a key local industry, especially in the central and southern areas, and after long hours down cramped and dangerous mineshafts and adits you can imagine the desire to relax and slake your thirst at the end of the day.

Although mining in the Peak District has a long history, and pubs have certainly played their part in its social history, rural inns are equally well associated with agriculture and animal husbandry. The name of the Drover's Arms in Glossop is a throwback to a time when large herds of animals would be driven sometimes long distances across country to market, with the drovers often staying at inns along the route.

The village pub or moorland inn has also been a place for farmers and shepherds to meet, and nowhere is this more evident over the years than at the Fox House Inn, high up on the moors above Sheffield. It began life in the 1770s as a two-roomed shepherd's cottage, and is not actually named after the animal as many suspect but almost certainly after George Fox of Callow Farm, near Hathersage, who built the place.

Records show that it was originally named the Traveller's Rest, most

A meeting place for shepherds and farmers for over 200 years, the Fox House Inn is a familiar landmark on the moors above Longshaw.

likely when it was first licensed in 1816. Like the Cat and Fiddle, the moorland inn is such a prominent and well-known feature, standing 1,132ft above sea level, that it has given its name to the location. It stood at a key junction of two important turnpikes (Dronfield to Chapel en le Frith, and Sheffield to Buxton), but during the nineteenth century it was also used by the Duke of Rutland to house his shooting guests when nearby Longshaw Lodge became full up. (His visitors to Longshaw included King George V and the Duke of Wellington, but I suspect that they weren't offered B&B at the local pub.)

Today owned by a national pub chain, the Fox House Inn has long been a popular tourist destination, and there are some fascinating stories from a time when horse-drawn carts and coaches (and flocks of sheep) rather than cars and motorbikes filled the yard outside. Because of its situation off the Burbage valley amid the rough grazing and purple heather moors, the inn once housed local shepherds – indeed according to one source it was briefly called the Shepherd's Rest. In especially rough winter weather it was not uncommon for straw to be strewn on the floor of the tap room so that the sheep could take overnight shelter as well as the shepherds!

During the 1890s the Duke of Rutland is said to have provided free refreshments for farmers and shepherds attending the annual sheep gatherings; but regardless of this, sheep were important business on the moors around Longshaw and Fox House. Before the animals were turned out for winter pasturing they had to be branded with the Duke's letter 'R', and since he took as many as 9,000 sheep each winter, there was a lot of work to do.

One story from 1880 describes how local shepherd Peter Priestley spent all day branding hundreds of sheep, and with the pitch still wet on his breeches called in at the Fox House for a pint or two on the way home. Tired out, he fell fast asleep in front of the fire with his legs crossed, only to wake some time later with his legs stuck together.

Below the shooting lodge at Longshaw is Longshaw Meadow where, every year since 1898, reputedly the oldest sheep dog trials in England are held. According to the often-told story, they came about following an argument in the Fox House Inn between farmers and shepherds over who owned the best sheepdog. Early on they played for stakes of quarts of beer, but before long it became serious business and a matter of professional pride.

The Longshaw estate is now owned by the National Trust, which has an information centre and tea room by the lodge, and from where there are paths which explore the edge of the Meadows, as well as the lovely sessile oak woodland of Padley Gorge.

Heading west now, and one of the oldest pubs in Whaley Bridge is the Shepherd's Arms on Old Road, off the main street. It was formerly a farmhouse when the town was probably no more than a modest village, and the attractive whitewashed pub almost certainly predates most of the other buildings around it. Situated on a slope, there are two outside terraces where you can sit and enjoy a pint, but for many the highlight is indoors where the traditional tap room has been lovingly-maintained, with stone flags and simple furnishings.

Shepherds are also remembered at the Packhorse Inn at Hayfield. Here it was customary for a 'shepherd's dinner' to be held on the first Saturday in July, before which there would be an auction in the car park of all the unclaimed stray sheep recently rounded up in the vicinity – then the proceeds would be spent in the pub.

Some pub names allude to various past times, practices and 'sports' now long consigned to history. The Bear at Alderwasley, an out-of-the-way hamlet located between Wirksworth and Whatstandwell, might possibly take its name from bear-baiting, since this was a common practice in some pub yards. The pub was recorded as the Brown Bear Inn in 1735, but as we will see in Chapter 7, animals in pub names can also have a religious or royal significance. A bear, for instance, was the crest of the Earls of Warwick and Leicester, although some of the pubs commemorating these esteemed families went by the full title of the Bear and Ragged Staff.

At Ashover, bear baiting regularly took pace outside the Black Swan. Travelling bear keepers, sometimes known as bearwards, usually stayed the night at the pub. At Matlock they lodged at the old Crown Hotel, and its cellars were used as pens for the bears.

A number of hostelries in the Peak are known to have had purpose-built cockpits where the equally unsavoury spectacle of cock-fighting once took place. Like bull and bear baiting, cock fighting was all about gambling, and it was popular with all classes of society.

Although there is no evidence that it ever took place at Sheldon, Disley and Whaley Bridge, the bird is still celebrated at the three locations by pubs called the Cock and Pullet, the Cock Inn and the Dandy Cock respectively. (The Dandy Cock is a localised name for a bantam fowl – also known as a dandy-hen – and regarded as a spirited fighter.) What is certain, though, is that there was certainly a pit behind the Hanging Gate pub on the edge of Chapel-en-le-Frith, and Ordnance Survey maps still refer to this area as Cockyard.

Not every pub bearing the name or picture of a cock bird denoted cock-fighting, however. In the seventeenth century something known as cock-ale could sometimes be found for sale, which was ale mixed with the jelly of minced meat of a boiled cock. Thankfully, pub fare has improved considerably since those days. Although cockfighting has long been illegal, it was finally banned in Britain in 1849 its legacy lingers on. Not only are there pubs still bearing the name, but the brewers Courage still have a cockerel as their symbol.

Getting together

Public houses, as their name suggests, have always been important as venues for local people to come together on neutral territory to enjoy some social interaction and discuss the issues of the day. Whether it was lead miners, farmhands or mill workers unwinding after a hard day's work, a drink and a chat in the 'local' has always been an important part of everyday life, cementing the role of the pub or inn in the social fabric of many Peak District communities.

In the next chapter we will see how the miners' Barmote Courts often chose to meet in village pubs; but in addition to this many other local groups and institutions came together at inns and pubs, as indeed plenty still do today. In the time before most small towns had purpose-built venues, the local magistrates court would sometimes meet in a function room of the leading inn. Examples include the Green Man and Black's Head Royal Hotel in Ashbourne, and the Royal Oak at Chapel en le Frith.

Pubs were also the meeting places of friendly societies, which began to appear at the end of the 1700s in an effort to help the less well-off and supplement the Poor Laws. These groups, sometimes known as Benefit Clubs, often had grandiose and occasionally bizarre names, but their intentions were honourable, and they played an important part in making the lives of the needy a little more bearable and providing financial support to ordinary people in times of need. A pub originally called the Prince's Arms (also known as the Paper Mill Inn) at Whitehough, north west of Chapel, was the meeting place of the Whitehough Victoria Lodge of Oddfellows, formed in 1830. They continued to meet right up until 1970, and today the handsome, eighteenth-century pub is called the Oddfellows Arms in their honour.

The Duke of York at Elton also hosted the Oddfellows, and here the Lodge was known as the Loyal Faithful Shepherd (there was even a

The Foresters Friendly Society parading past the Ordnance Arms Hotel in Hathersage, probably in the early 1900s, as part of their annual pilgrimage to Little John's Grave at the parish church. The pub was later renamed the Hathersage Inn and is now closed.

junior branch for boys under 16 called the Loyal Lamb Lodge!). The Elton Local History Group has recently published a fascinating booklet all about this Lodge, which was established in 1842, and it includes extracts from original documents and a wonderful photo of Lodge members with their banner and staffs lined up outside the pub in 1895. (Copies are on sale in the pub.)

The Duke of York was not unusual, since many pubs had club rooms where local societies met, and at a time well before the National Health Service these voluntary groups were sometimes known as 'sick clubs'. One of the most impressively-named orders was the Humane Friendly Indefatigable Union Society, which had branches in Tideswell and elsewhere. The Independent Friendly Society at Crich met '…for the benefit of sick and infirm members' and their early venue was the Black Swan public house.

The Women's Conversational Club came together in a Bakewell alehouse, while the Masons and Foresters convened elsewhere in the town. Then there was the Loyal Lily of the Valley Lodge at Hope, the Inkerman at Great Longstone, Wensley Jubilee Friendly Society and the Loyal Welcome Traveller of the Peak Lodge at Bradwell.

Although many of these mutual benefit societies have now disappeared, or live on in name only, some still meet and organise fundraising events for local charities. For instance, the Royal Antediluvian Order of Buffaloes (commonly known as 'the Buffs') still occasionally meet at the Farmyard Inn at Youlgrave and the Duke William at Matlock.

However, pubs are about more than just a chat over a pint. Music and dance has often played an important role, and some pubs and inns are noted for their live entertainment. The Fishpond Hotel at Matlock Bath (see Chapter 8) has regular gigs at its upstairs ballroom, and there are also frequent live performances at the Wheatsheaf at Bakewell, Barley Mow at Bonsall, Kings Arms at Chapel – to name but a few.

Several pubs have weekly or fortnightly jazz sessions, including the Traveller's Rest at Flash Bar, Scotsman's Pack at Hathersage and the George at Hayfield; and folk evenings occur at, among other places, the Packhorse Inn at Little Longstone, the Manners Hotel at Bakewell and the Olde Cheshire Cheese at Castleton.

Hunting, shooting and fishing

With its vast expanses of heather moorland and its well-stocked streams and rivers, the Peak District is renowned for outdoor sports, such as grouse shooting and fishing. However, historically-speaking perhaps the oldest blood sports association is hunting itself, since from Norman times much of the Peak was a royal hunting ground. The names of many Peakland pubs, as well as some of their histories, reflect this age-old pursuit.

There are three 'Sportsman' pubs in our region, all of which are found in the Dark Peak close to or virtually on the important grouse-shooting moors. There's a Sportsman's Arms at Strines, a mile south east of Marple, at the foot of the uplands ringing the Goyt valley; while the Sportsman at Rivelin is on the edge of the moors high on Sheffield's western fringe.

Its namesake at Hayfield is located on the road from the village to Kinder Reservoir, and close to Bowden Bridge quarry where many of the protesters on the celebrated Kinder Scout Mass Trespass of 1932 met before setting off. Their actions were an attempt to gain public access to the huge swathes of private moorland which stretched across the highest and wildest part of the Peak District, and which at that time were managed solely for shooting. It may seem incredible to today's generation of walkers and climbers that back then virtually the whole of the Dark Peak uplands were out of bounds, especially as 2004 has seen the opening up of even more mountain and moorland under the Countryside and Rights of Way (CROW) Act.

So, as you settle back in the comfortable surroundings of the Sportsman at Hayfield, you can reflect on just how radically things have changed in little more than 80 years – from privately-run moorland shoots peppered with 'keep out' notices through to officially-designated 'Access Land' with welcoming signs and codes of conduct.

There are plenty of other pub names which continue the theme of hunting and shooting. The Poacher's Inns at Bollington and at Hope recall one particular nefarious aspect, while there are Grouse Inns at Birch Vale, Chunal Moor (south of Glossop), Darley Dale and Longshaw. You can sup at the Cock and Pheasant, also at Bollington, or go elsewhere in this large and pub-rich Cheshire village for the Dog and Partridge (which also appears at the other end of the Peak District in Thorpe, and on the A628 west of Langsett). There's also a Hare and Hounds at Birch Vale.

Hunting has a close association with country pubs – just look at the number of thematic prints and replica hunting horns which adorn the walls of rural inns. Many hunts met at village pubs, including the Duke of York at Elton where huge joints of meat were roasted to feed the hungry participants. And it is no coincidence that the brewers Tetley have a red-coated huntsman for their logo.

In terms of names, there's the Roebuck Inn at Chapel en le Frith, the town's traditional and handsome market pub. Three Stags Heads can be found at both Wardlow Mires and at Darley Bridge, by the River Derwent north of Matlock. The latter is a tastefully maintained, eighteenth-century building, with the letters 'GOQ' carved above the main door. Apparently they stand for 'Go out quietly', and if you do you may be treated to the sight of deer feeding at the far end of the beer garden, since a small herd of roe roam wild among the wooded hills towards Winster and Bonsall.

There are quite a few pubs where a set of antlers or horns still adorn the walls, and there are others where you might meet stranger things too – most of them long deceased. At the Bull i' th' Thorn on the A515 there's what purports to be a bear's head in a glass case; while the aforementioned Three Stags Heads at Wardlow Mires is renowned for its petrified cat which sits in a case near the fireplace (petrified in more ways than one, judging by the expression on its face); plus there's a stuffed mountain hare, in its distinctive white winter coat, in a box behind the bar.

At the Strines Inn near Bradfield you can find a stuffed sparrowhawk and golden plover staring lifelessly at you from behind glass; while at the Little Mill Inn at Rowarth there is a large glass case near the main door showing three furry mammals. The two smaller chaps are definitely grey squirrels, but according to the landlady the third is a possum. Make up your own mind on that one.

Perhaps the pub with the most stuffed animals is the Crag Inn at Wildboarclough. This isolated hamlet – known locally as 'Wilbercluff' – sits in the narrow valley below Shutlingsloe, a large and distinctive conical hill off the A54 Buxton-Congleton road. The pub is located near the start of the popular path up to its 1,659ft summit, and what better, after a few hours vigorous exercise and a battering from a sharp westerly, than a thirst-quenching pint and a plate of something hot in this distinctive Cheshire hostelry?

The building itself began life as a seventeenth-century farmhouse originally called Bottom o'th' Bank, until it became an inn in the 1830s. Around that time, this seemingly remote community was actually the centre of a flourishing textile industry, with Clough Brook harnessed to power a 30-foot water wheel which helped power a small calico-printing unit. Despite switching to carpet production, inevitably it couldn't keep up with the factory competition further afield, and all that remains today is Stanley Pool, the artificial reservoir behind the church, built to power the water wheel, and further up the lane, the forlorn grandeur of Crag Mill.

The name of Wildboarclough also tells a story, and I suppose it sort of ties in with 'ex-animals'. There's actually a pub called the Wild Boar further along the A54 towards Congleton (near Allgreave), and the name of this former coaching inn refers to England's indigenous and now extinct wild pig, the last one of which was supposedly killed around here in the fifteenth century.

At that time, this area would have formed part of Macclesfield Forest, kept solely as the hunting preserve of the nobility and well-to-do – echoes from a more modern era of the jealously-guarded grouse moors further north perhaps? The Steward of Macclesfield Forest imposed strict Forest Laws that were harsh and unforgiving. You could lose an arm for poaching – if you were lucky, that is – and there were also penalties if you were caught collecting firewood or let your animals stray into the forest. Among the animals hunted were almost certainly the wild boar, and mounted on a wall inside the Wild Boar Inn is the head, tusks and skin of a boar – with a bullet hole in its right flank.

Fishing is also represented by Peak pubs, most notably the Angler's Rest at Bamford and Miller's Dale, the Lazy Trout at Meerbrook, near Tittesworth Reservoir, and the Grouse and Claret at Rowsley (it's the name of a fishing fly – see Chapter 7).

Across the River Derwent from the Grouse and Claret is the historic Peacock Hotel which, like the Square and Compass at Darley Bridge, is one of several pubs in the Peak District to boast its own fishing rights. In the case of the Peacock it's a seven-mile stretch of the River Wye upstream to Bakewell through the Haddon Hall estate, and is popular with fly fishermen seeking trout (rainbow and brown) and grayling. In fact, the Derbyshire Wye is famous for its strain of breeding rainbow trout, and the Peacock Hotel hires rods and sells flies and other equipment for visiting anglers.

According to the hotel's promotional booklet, 'almost any fly pattern can be successful on the Wye… as the free-rising rainbow trout will often provide sport through the day'. The dry flies have wonderful names, with 'May flies' including Green Drake, Grey Drake and Spent Gnat, while the 'Traditionals' number Sherry Spinner, Lunns Particular and Grey Duster, and the 'Moderns' include Blue Winged Olive, Pale Morning Dun and Elk Hair Caddis.

Two people who would have felt quite at home amid dry flies and rods in Derbyshire would be Izaak Walton and Charles Cotton, the famous seventeenth-century-fishermen cum philosophers who are remembered in the names of pubs either end of their beloved Dovedale (see Chapter 4).

Traditional pub games

It's inevitable that a lot of pubs change as they get sold or taken over, and modernisation can certainly improve some places. But for many traditionalists the spread of flashing fruit machines, piped music and karaoke evenings have ruined the atmosphere and appearance of some fine old establishments. Thankfully there are still a number of pubs across the Peak District where you can sit and enjoy a quiet conversation, and some still retain a few traditional pub games which have been enjoyed in the inns and taverns of this country for hundreds of years.

Many pubs have their own teams for various sports and activities. Darts and pool are two of the most common, plus there are numerous pub quiz leagues. Some pubs have their own football and cricket teams, and the Bull's Head at Monyash even has its own netball side.

The French game of boules has established itself at a number of pubs, and most take part in competitive leagues. You can find outdoor boules pitches at the Farmyard Inn (Youlgrave), Rising Sun (Middleton by Wirksworth) and the Old Bowling Green (Winster). There's also a floodlit boules pitch across the road from the Malt Shovel on Wirksworth Moor, and the car park adjoining it used to be a lawn tennis court.

It's hard to imagine many pubs having their own tennis court these days (nor pub-goers necessarily wanting to play tennis over a pint, for that matter); but the Ram's Head at Disley does own two crown bowling greens behind the pub, upon which visitors can try their hand at a game. The Bowling Green pub at Ashbourne is named after the green that could once be found next door; and presumably the afore-mentioned Old Bowling Green at Winster, as well as the Olde Bowling Green at Bradwell, must have had similar facilities in the past.

The more genteel indoors pursuit of bar billiards, which is thought to have originated from the popular nineteenth-century pub game bagatelle, is still quite popular in southern England, but in the Peak District, few tables remain. The Little John Hotel in Hathersage still has one, and a fine example can still be viewed tucked away in the corner of the Lathkil Hotel at Over Haddon.

Another traditional English pub game which has sadly almost died out in the Peak District is skittles, or nine pins, the forerunner of ten-pin bowling, where wooden balls are rolled down a lane to knock over skittles. It still takes place at the Royal Oak (Tansley) and Red Lion (Kniveton). However, a miniature version of this game called bar or table skittles still exists at a few pubs, such as the Duke William at Matlock, the Butcher's Arms at Reaps Moor south of Longnor, and the Plough Inn at Flagg (which also has a bar billiards table).

The gentle pursuit of dominoes still carries on in a few of the more traditional Peakland pubs, such as the George Hotel at Youlgrave, and it's a game that hasn't changed that much since the Chinese first played it in the fourteenth century. It arrived in Britain in the late eighteenth century from France, possibly via French prisoners of war, and the word 'domino' is French for the black and white hood worn by priests in winter.

Did you know that cribbage is the only card game that can legally be played for money in English pubs? Cribbage, or crib, has its roots in a Tudor game called 'Noddy', and was made famous by the seventeenth-century poet and gambler Sir John Suckling, who managed to cheat most of England's wealthy aristocracy out of their money by distributing packs of marked cards then beating them at cribbage.

The King's Head in Bonsall has an original gaming table, and there's another old one at the Quiet Woman at Earl Sterndale. In a more general sense, old-fashioned pub games are possibly remembered in the name of the Board Inn in Whaley Bridge – although it may well have more to do with general hospitality for visiting stagecoach passengers (board of fare).

Another traditional pub game which is rarely seen these days is shove ha'penny. It was the younger brother of a game called shovel board, versions of which have been played in taverns for over 400 years. Basically, the coins were pushed along a board with the intention of landing them within horizontal lines or 'beds' – three coins in one bed in a single turn was called a 'sergeant' and five a 'sergeant major'. King Henry VIII was even said to be keen on the game.

Over the centuries the game has been called according to the type of coin used, so that the 'shoffe-grote' was popular under the reign of Edward IV when the coins used were groats. A version of the game called push-penny is still played in the pubs of Stamford in Lincolnshire, still using three old English pennies.

A far more unusual and little-known pub game is called 'Aunt Sally' and involves players throwing batons at a wooden skittle known as a doll. It was possibly established by Royalist soldiers during the English Civil war when King Charles resided in Oxford; indeed, the small number of pubs that still play the game are all based in Oxfordshire and they even have their own Aunt Sally league. (A pub called the Derbyshire Sally once existed in Winster, curiously enough.)

Likewise, there is a 'bat and trap' league in Kent, where pubs compete in an outdoor competition which is like a bizarre version of cricket. The trap is a mechanical device which shoots a ball into the air, and the batsmen then has to hit the ball between two posts 21 yards away.

Other, rather more sedate, indoor pub games include pub quoits and pitch penny – the simple tossing of coins at a hole in a bench or wall. Similar to this is the frog game, still played on the continent, where discs or coins are thrown at different sized holes in a piece of furniture. In England it is known as toad in the hole, there being just the one size object and only one hole. Apparently it's still played in a few pubs in Sussex. A glance at the sophisticated fruit and quiz machines in some of today's pubs shows just how far things have changed.

Golf is not necessarily a game that you associate with pubs, nor are there many golf courses in the Peak District. Normally you would expect to retire to the clubhouse bar after a morning's round, but rather unusually the Robin Hood Inn near Baslow created its own six-hole course on ground to the rear of the pub. Meanwhile, on the edge of the course which occupies a large part of Fairfield Common at Buxton, you can find the splendidly-named 19th Hole public house. Sadly, not many golfers appear to patronise it.

Preserving a forgotten way of life

Luckily for pub-goers, the wide variety of Peak District inns cater for just about everyone – from the tourist honeypots to the trendy town centre bars, the family dining pubs on the main roads to the busy village locals and posh hotels. But despite the Peak District's rural character, it's hard to imagine that there are many pubs that have not been touched in some way by the commercial and marketing forces of the twenty-first century.

Around 38,000 people live within the boundaries of the Peak District National Park (not including Ashbourne, Matlock, Glossop and Buxton), but as many as 22 million day visits are made each year, making it the second most visited national park in the world.

It's tempting, therefore, to imagine that pubs in this region would simply not be able to survive without succumbing in some way to the pressures of such a top visitor destination. After all, most either serve meals or offer some sort of accommodation; and for many pubs in the more out of the way locations with a relatively small local audience, this provides the crucial income which determines whether they get by or go to the wall.

However, even amid the bustling throng of summer visitors which clogs the streets of Bakewell and Castleton and cause pedestrian traffic jams on the stepping stones of Dovedale, there are still a handful of pubs which have refused to yield to the demands of the modern pub industry, and remain as beacons from the past – traditional and unspoilt in appearance and attitude.

Indeed, it can come as a breath of fresh air in this age where national chain pubs, in particular, employ professionals to 'make over' their pubs and give them the 'olde worlde' feel, complete with the obligatory agricultural implements from yesteryear, plus rows of dusty-looking old books actually stuck together and screwed to the shelf!

The Duke of York is the village pub of Elton, a former leadmining community located off the B5056 mid-way between Bakewell and Matlock. Although there's still a good café which opens at weekends, the shops have all gone and even the youth hostel recently closed. Despite this, Elton retains its village school, and the community spirit is such that it even won the 2004 Derbyshire Village of the Year competition. It's a peaceful sort of place, much loved by weekend walkers and cyclists, with lovely views across to Robin Hood's Stride and Stanton Moor.

You would think that the situation would be ripe for an enterprising village pub offering bed and breakfast and evening meals, possibly with some self-catering rooms at the back. Not a bit of it. The Duke of York has waved it all away, and remains a true local pub where local people go to have a drink and socialise. It's not an unfriendly or unwelcoming place, although rumour has it that once upon a time, Friday nights in the pub were locally understood to be for men of the village only. Rather, it has refused to yield to the modern pub culture that sees tables laid and numbered for diners before they cross the threshold, and where a trip across the back yard to the loo is something that some pub-goers have only read about.

The pub sits opposite the village church, and is demonstrably unshowy. The exterior simply has the name of the pub – not a swinging sign, just a board – attached to the front wall. There are no picnic tables and parasols, nor any overflowing hanging baskets bursting with colour. This is a basic and unspoilt village local which doesn't dress itself up for the tourist market, and as such is one of the few pubs in the region which feature in CAMRA's 'National Inventory of Pub Interiors of Outstanding Heritage Interest'.

CAMRA (the Campaign for Real Ale) launched the initiative in order to create a permanent record of truly historic public houses, from unspoilt rural pubs to grand Victorian glass and tile palaces, and to help foster public awareness and support for their preservation. Pubs on the list have by and large remained unaltered for the past half century, and the Duke of York exemplifies a number of characteristics which show how little the building and its interior has changed.

It's a relatively plain, Victorian stone building, with sparsely-furnished front rooms and a cosier tap room at the back where the bar is situated. This small and attractive room features wooden panelling and fitted seats, a tiled floor and a huge stone fireplace. There's a serving hatch from the bar into the corridor, probably designed for off-sales but useful for when things get a little crowded; while above the bar is a glazed screen behind which the glasses are stacked. Steps at the far end of the corridor lead to a door into the yard – the toilets are on the far side of this.

That the pub has stayed virtually unaltered is mostly due to the fact that it has remained in the same hands for the past 37 years. The land-lady, Mary Elliott, sees no need for music when there's decent conversation to be had; and although there's some confectionery on sale behind the bar, the pub does not serve food, something that makes it almost unique in the Peak District. Because there's no need to pander to diners, the pub doesn't actually open until 8.30pm in the evening (this is probably why some people think that it's closed down and go elsewhere).

Another Peak District pub which features on CAMRA's National Inventory is the Barley Mow at Kirk Ireton. The last surviving pub in the village, which is located three miles south of Wirksworth, the Barley Mow can be found on Main Street and is a three-storey, grade II* listed stone building which is believed to have been built as a farmhouse. Mostly Jacobean, there's an old sundial under the centre eaves which bears the date 1683.

Inside, the three simply furnished rooms either sport a tiled or parquet floor, are heated by open fires or stoves, and the basic furniture includes slate tables made from the four quarters of a former billiards

The Barley Mow at Kirk Ireton, near Wirksworth, is a lovely Jacobean building in the centre of the village.

Beer is still served straight from racked barrels at the Barley Mow.

table. There are no fruit machines nor piped music, and the beer is racked up in barrels behind the bar in the traditional manner.

The previous landlady was Lily Ford, who spent her entire life – all 89 years of it – at the Barley Mow. Lily was very much from the old school, and was adamant that traditions would be maintained and no truck would be given to these silly modern ideas. In 1971 she resisted decimalisation and up until she died in 1976 insisted that customers pay in 'old' money.

Mary Short, who took over that same year, has carried on in her wake, preserving the timeless character of this lovely village pub. There are filled rolls at lunchtime, and traditional cider is also on sale, but it is the sight of the racked barrels lined up at the back of the small bar – instead of hidden away in the cellar – that is particularly eye-catching.

Whereas the Barley Mow has the air of a well-to-do village farm-house, the Three Stags Heads at Wardlow Mires is an altogether different proposition, and probably reflects its remote and exposed location. The 300-year-old cottage, plain to the point of drab from outside, has also served as a farm, and with its stone-flagged floor and handsome, black-leaded range it remains gloriously unspoilt; indeed, there was not even a proper counter until the present one was installed in the 1950s.

The doorway is straight off the busy A623 (Chesterfield to Chapel road), opposite the petrol station by the Ashford turning, and just crossing the main road to the pub can be hazardous enough. You enter straight into the small, simple bar, which doesn't take many to get crowded, and here the place comes into its own. The room on the right is a relatively new addition, but both are kept very basic and no frills, with wooden benches and settles, and a scattering of stools gathered around scrubbed wooden tables.

The pub is determinedly authentic and has refused to bow to modern trends, as demonstrated on a number of counts. Whereas many pubs now ban dogs outright, the Three Stags Heads has no such qualms, and a pack of lurchers belonging to Geoff Fuller, the long-serving licensee, are nearly always to be found pattering around the floor or curled up on the seats.

The approach to serving beer and lager is even more unique, with basically plenty of the former and none of the latter. Aside from Guinness, there are usually four real ales on offer, supplied by Abbeydale brewery of Sheffield. The 'house' beer is, most appropriately, called Black Lurcher, and at an ABV of a whopping 8 per cent, it is not for the faint hearted. As it says on the pump badge: 'Its bite is worse than its bark'.

Although there's wine and spirits behind the bar, as you would expect, there is no lager tap in sight, and a notice at the side of the bar spells out the establishment's position in no uncertain terms: 'PLEASE don't ask the landlord for DRAUGHT LAGER as a smack in the gob may cause offence'. Don't say you haven't been warned.

However, if all this gives the impression that the Three Stags Heads is a hostile and unwelcoming place, then you would be mistaken. It's a pub that is exactly what it sets out to be: traditional, simple and unfussy. In general, it's open from Friday evening to Sunday lunchtime only, although it has been known to open midweek; but freshly-prepared hot food dishes are available, usually featuring locally-caught game including pheasant and rabbit (and served on crockery actually made in the barn-turned-pottery out the back – individual items are also for sale). There's even a small dining room on the left as you enter that you can book in advance. On Saturday evenings folk musicians often gather in the second room for an impromptu session, and with the fire roaring and the conversation buzzing it can be a lively place. Only don't ask for a pint of draught lager.

Two other pubs fall into this broad category, perhaps best summed up as 'timeless'; although whether time will be called on these places by the time you read this book is another matter. The Red Lion at Wensley, between Winster and Darley Dale, was once a coaching inn on the route to Matlock and has been in the hands of the Belfield family since 1949. George Belfield and his sister Barbara currently run the pub, and George vividly remembers helping his father manage the adjoining farm while his mother and sister ran the pub.

The pub has remained largely unaltered over the decades, with Formica tables and pub memorabilia from a time when Guinness was good for you and Double Diamond worked wonders. There's no draught beer or lager, only bottles; and the pub is renowned for its home-made milkshakes, including the 'Milliguin' made out of half a pint of milk and half a pint of Guinness.

The Royal Cottage is a pub that has given its name to the location, on a junction of the A53 high up on the bleak Staffordshire Moorlands above Leek. It was once described by an old guidebook I came across as 'uninviting', but I suspect that colourful hanging baskets and even picnic tables wouldn't last long in this windswept environment.

It's a solid old building, dark and sombre as the gritstone moors which surround it, and in appearance like a small and not particularly profitable farmstead. Most people whizzing past in their cars on the busy Leek-Buxton road probably don't even register the austere building, since it's one of several huddled by the roadside. In fact, you have to look quite closely in order to work out that it is actually a public house, for the only indication is a modest sign above the door – there's nothing in the windows or on the door, nor even a traditional swinging board.

The pub's name refers to the advance to Derby – and ignominious retreat to Scotland – of Bonnie Prince Charlie's army in 1745. The Young Pretender is supposed to have slept in the pub (on a settee under the back window to be precise); and if he or his followers stepped into the Royal Cottage today they probably wouldn't be too unfamiliar with the surroundings. However, Olive Prince – who has run the pub single-handed since 1961 – would quite rightly insist on decent manners and discourage any thoughts of plundering or pillaging.

It's one of those places where, as you walk in, you have the uncanny feeling of entering someone's private room. Sure, there is a small bar, but there are also armchairs and a settee covered by old throws, plus an open fire. There's also a side room, which is handy on Friday evenings (the pub only opens at weekends) since it is often crowded with folk musicians. The décor, it has to be said, is basic and no-frills, with fake brick wallpaper above the fireplace that must surely be several decades old.

It's a pub which won't appeal to large numbers of people, since you come here to drink and talk, and perhaps listen to some live music. There's no kiddies' play area, no wine list, nor do you have to wait by the door to be seated and give your table number at the bar. It's authentic and honest, but how long it will last into the twenty-first century is the big question.

3
All in a Day's Work

Farming and rural matters

The Peak District remains an overwhelmingly rural environment, dotted by villages and small towns such as Bakewell and Matlock. It's fringed by larger settlements, like Ashbourne and Glossop, and then the cities of Derby, Manchester and Sheffield (in fact part of the Peak District National Park actually lies within Sheffield's city boundary).

The region's pubs reflect this situation, with a mixture of village inns and town taverns, and the names and histories of these establishments can tell us a lot about the everyday lives of the men and women who have lived and worked the Peak for generations.

Although tourism has usurped agriculture as the major local employer, farming is still a strong historical theme when it comes to pub names. The Wheatsheaf is common, found in Bakewell, Baslow, Dove Holes and Wirksworth, and you might not be too surprised to discover that three golden wheatsheaves appear on the coat of arms belonging to the Worshipful Company of Bakers (as it has done since 1486). It also has an heraldic reference to the Earls of Exeter.

The rural theme is continued with the Barley Mow, the name given to a rick of barley from which ale used to be brewed (apparently the 'mow' should rhyme with 'cow'). Such a sign was sometimes used simply to indicate that beer was sold from the building. There are two fine pubs of this name in the south of the Peak, at Bonsall and Kirk Ireton, both of which are featured in more detail in other chapters.

Although today the name of the Farmyard Inn at Youlgrave, near Bakewell, may seem out of place among the cottages and houses, 300 years ago it was indeed a farm building, which was converted into a pub in 1829. The low-slung ceiling, dark beams and grand open fireplace at the far end of the bar still give it an authentic feel with plenty of atmosphere, and on the walls are some fine old sepia-tinted photographs showing regulars lining up outside the pub in yesteryear. I've also heard it said that, strangely enough, it is the only pub with this name in the entire country, which is one of those things that is almost impossible to verify.

Regulars mark Coronation Day with a group photo outside the Farmyard Inn at Youlgrave.

The Plough is another familiar pub name, found at Ashbourne, Two Dales (north of Matlock), Flagg and Hathersage. 'Plough Monday' was the first Monday after the 12 days of Christian celebration at Christmas, and represented the beginning of the new agricultural year. Ploughs would be decorated and hauled through the village to raise 'plough money' for what was known as an ale frolic. But while it usually refers to the agricultural implement, sometimes the pub sign can depict the seven bright stars in the constellation Ursa Major (which are also known, rather intriguingly, as Charles's Wain – a wain being a farm wagon or cart).

Moving logically on to matters equine, the Monsal Head Hotel, although historically catering for the tourists who once alighted from the train in the valley below (see later in this chapter), does have next to it a cosy bar situated in the former stable block. The appropriately-named Stables Bar once housed the animals that pulled the coaches and carts full of passengers and their luggage, and now the open, stone-flagged building contains seated areas grouped around the individual stalls, each of which are named after horses: Samson, Blossom, Captain and Betty. The bar is decorated by horse brasses and saddles, and in front of the warming stove is an original wooden pig bench (once used, as you might have guessed, for chopping up pig carcases).

Sheep-farming is still widespread in the Peak District, especially on the uplands, and the Fleece Inn at Holme, in West Yorkshire, and the

Ram's Head at Disley in Cheshire, are a reminder that for three centuries, wool was the mainstay of the English economy.

But surely the most common pub name we immediately associate with farming and the rural way of life is the Bull's Head. There are pubs of this name at Ashford in the Water, Buxton, Castleton, Foolow, Old Glossop, Hayfield, Kettleshulme, Monyash, Tintwistle, Wardlow and Youlgrave, making it one of the most popular pub names in this region. There's also an Old Bull's Head at Little Hucklow; and in Chapter 8 we will discover a whole lot more Bull's Heads that are

The Bull's Head is one of the most common pub names in the Peak District, and this fine stone relief can be found above the archway at Youlgrave's.

no longer pubs. So it's no wonder that as little as a century ago there were reported to be between twenty to thirty Bull's Heads in the Peak District.

Predictably enough, nearly all of them depict the picture of a huge great beast, and indeed many may simply have been named after the animal or have something to do with a market place or bull baiting. On the village green at Foolow, for instance, close to the Bull's Head pub is a surviving example of an original bull ring attached to a boulder; and Eyam's bull ring is on show in the Square near the Miner's Arms. Bull baiting also took place by the seventeenth-century village cross in the centre of Bonsall, outside the King's Head, although the bull ring itself is now kept in the local church. The reason that it resides in the church is that in 1834 the vicar, in a fit of compassion, paid a guinea to buy the bull so that it would be saved from baiting during the Wakes.

There are two other possible reasons why the Bull's Head was such a popular pub name. In the days before the Reformation it had a religious significance, referring not to the farmyard animal but to the Papal bull, since the seal of a monastery or collegiate body was known as La Boule (from the Latin *bulla*). A further explanation, not entirely unrelated, suggests that the Bull's Head moniker was a sort of code, denoting that the establishment had royalist sympathies.

Among the various Bull's Heads dotted about the Peak District are some particularly attractive and interesting pubs. The one in the centre of Youlgrave has a wonderful carved stone relief of a snorting bull's head above the handsome coaching arch; while Ashford in the Water's is set back from the main street near the church, and originally opened as an alehouse in 1701 under the name the Turk's Head. Back then it stood at the edge of the village and was predominantly a farm.

Indeed, it was quite common in those days for the rural pub to be part of a wider family business, such as a farm. The husband may well have been running the farm or shoeing horses, while the wife looked after the selling of drink. Now, of course, the pub is itself the core business, and in the case of the Bull's Head at Ashford, it has become well-known for its high-quality bar meals.

The national census of 1851 found that of 22,082 farmers, over 1,500 were innkeepers and a further 1,898 'beershop keepers'. There are numerous examples of publicans holding down other occupations. In Peter Fellows's absorbing book *Bonsall at Work* (part of the Bonsall History Project) we learn that James Briddon was the landlord of the Via Gellia Inn, which later became the Pig o'Lead Inn. In addition to the pub, he also ran a thriving blacksmith's business in the cottage across the road. At the nearby Barley Mow, landlord Jesse Bunting was also a spar miner; and at the King's Head, Isaac Doxey was a joiner for almost 40 years. In 1860, George Statham is recorded as 'a butcher and innkeeper' at the Miner's Standard, which once stood on Bonsall High Street, but by the 1920s this pub, like several others in the village, had closed. (See Chapter 8 for more details of lost pubs.)

The Gate Inn at Tansley was also run as a farm, and stayed in the same family for two centuries until 1900. The Anchor Inn at Tideswell was originally a farmstead, as was the original building on the site now occupied by the Waterloo Inn at Taddington; and the Bluebell Inn at Tissington was a working farm until as recently as the 1940s, when landowner Sir Henry Fitzherbert of nearby Tissington Hall converted it into a pub.

Records from the 1860s show that the George Hotel at Hathersage contained a hay loft and cowhouse, in addition to the coach house and stabling for eight horses. The landlord at the Star Inn at Taddington (now closed) used to be a saddle and harness maker; while the name of the Square and Compass inn at Darley Bridge alludes to the tools of the stonemasons who worked in places like the nearby Stancliffe quarries (as well as having a connection with the freemasons). Meanwhile, the Old Bowling Green at Smalldale in Bradwell – an alehouse since the 1500s – also doubled up as a local slaughterhouse; while the name of another pub from the same village – the Shoulder of Mutton – is surely also a throwback to those times.

Today there are just one or two of the less 'touristy', out-of-the way rural inns where the business of running a pub still goes hand in hand with some small-scale farming. The Red Lion at Wensley, referred to in the previous chapter, is one example, as is the Quiet Woman at Earl Sterndale, where you can still buy eggs from the pub's hens across the bar.

The aforementioned Bear Inn at Alderwasley has been both a farmhouse and alehouse in its long and chequered existence, and often at the same time. In 1851 the tenant was recorded as a Mr William Clarke, 'victualler and farmer of 16 acres'. In July 1920 the Alderwasley estate was sold off by the Hurt family, the local landowners, and that included the Bear Inn. A copy of the auction notice is framed on the wall of the present pub, with Lot 38 including the house and four acres, a well of water, range of piggeries, calf pen, cowhouses, hay store and cart shed.

Other professions which publicans might have held down included wheelwrights and coopers, the latter making barrels used in, among other things, the pub trade; but sadly neither of these appear to be remembered in Peak District pub names. However, we do have a Jolly Carter, who smiles down benevolently from a pub sign in Chapel en le Frith.

As was the case in Bonsall, some publicans were also blacksmiths, at a time when virtually every village had its own smithy. There are plenty of pubs in the Peak which celebrate this line of work, including Smith's Tavern on St John Street in Ashbourne. Squeezed between modern shops, the building dates from the 1680s, and as unlikely as it sounds, originally had a monastic purpose as lodgings for religious visitors. The back room even has the original bishop's chair, along with a few other splendid period furnishings.

While some of the pubs in the centre of Ashbourne have lost a little (and some a great deal) of their original character thanks to over-vigorous refurbishment, it's probably true to say that the interior of Smith's Tavern remains authentic and largely untarnished. It really is an old-fashioned town tavern; but despite the picture of a blacksmith at work on the sign outside there's not an anvil in sight.

However, one pub which can certainly lay its credentials on the bar with pride is the Leathers Smithy in Langley, south east of Macclesfield in Cheshire. This eighteenth-century building was formerly a blacksmiths and is named after William Leather, a local farrier who became the first licensee in 1821 (you can see a picture of the chap on the pub's menu).

The place is located just to the east of the village by Ridgegate Reservoir, and it is well worth nosing out. Popular with diners, it also offers a seated area around an open fire on a stone-flagged floor, providing a welcome spot for booted walkers who enjoy the paths over Tegg's Nose and through Macclesfield Forest.

Not too far away, on the A54 Buxton-Congleton road at the hamlet of Allgreave, the former smithy at the Rose and Crown has been turned into the pub's function room. The pub was built as a turnpike inn, and as well as the toll house, the smithy must have been kept busy shoeing the extra horses required for the long pull up on to the moors.

Other pub names refer not so much to the blacksmith as his four-footed charge. The Horseshoe Inn at Longnor dates from 1609 and is a reminder that for a long time its customers would turn up either on horses or horse-drawn. There's another Horseshoe Inn at Matlock Green, as well as the Three Horseshoes at Spitewinter (on the Matlock-Chesterfield road on the eastern edge of the Peak) and at Blackshaw Moor, on the A53 Buxton Road approaching Leek.

Even though the Spitewinter pub sign depicts a game of horseshoe-throwing, the name presumably refers to the plight of the horse-drawn traveller, with the missing fourth horseshoe being the reason that the blacksmith, and possibly the pub, was engaged.

The miner's lot

Along with farming, the other important traditional industry of the Peak District has been mining. There are still quite a few active mines and quarries, although lead extraction has been replaced by limestone (mostly aggregate for roads) and gritstone for decorative building work, plus some fluorspar is removed for the chemical industry.

Associations with the industry are still very close in some places, and that includes pubs. The small village of Birchover, for example, backs on to Stanton Moor and several gritstone quarries, and in the Red Lion on the main street you can enjoy a lunchtime snack called 'the Quarryman's Lunch' (rather than the more familiar Ploughman's).

However, it is lead that made the Peak District famous, and its legacy stretches back two millennia when the Romans laid one of their character-istically straight roads (now the A515) in order to link their settlement of *Aquae Arnemetiae* (Buxton) with the centre of their lead mining industry at the still-to-be conclusively identified place called *Lutudarum*.

Derbyshire is the only lead mining county recorded in the Domesday Book, although the heyday of lead mining was not until the eighteenth century when as many as 10,000 miners were employed. But the lead veins were often difficult to work, and the mines prone to flooding, and by 1901 less than 300 lead miners were left in Derbyshire.

Today lead mining has been consigned to the history books, but if you look carefully as you tour the White Peak, you can still see tell-tale signs from the past. The odd bumps and grassed-over hollows spread around the fields are often the remains of old excavations and spoil tips, while here and there you will spot occasional chimneys and ruined mine buildings. The best-preserved of these is Magpie Mine near Sheldon, west of Bakewell, where the Peak District Mines Historical Society has carefully preserved the original engine house, chimneys and winding gear.

Not far away from Sheldon is Lathkill Dale, today a tranquil limestone dale much loved by walkers and naturalists, but once it echoed to the sounds of lead mining, with steam engines, a 50 foot-high water wheel and mile-long drainage tunnels known as soughs constructed in an effort to drain the water and make the mines more viable. At the head of the dale lies the village of Monyash, and it was in the Bull's Head overlooking the green that – drinking aside – much of the important mining business was conducted.

The Bull's Head is the sole survivor of what were once five pubs in Monyash. It is a spacious and solid, seventeenth-century stone building, part of which is a three-storey affair. Next to it the former blacksmiths has been converted into a café, and both this and the pub are well-run and popular with locals and visitors alike.

Two centuries or so ago the Bull's Head would have been particularly well frequented, since it was the venue for a special miners' meeting known as the Barmote (sometimes spelt Barmoot) Court. It met usually once or twice a year, and adjudicated on disputes and contentious claims, settling disagreements over who had the right to work a specific vein.

Indeed, the freeing, giving and selling of mines was an integral function of the Barmote Court, presided over by the Barmaster. If a mine was considered idle and unworked, the Barmaster would cut a nick in the wooden winding gear (the stowe) at the top of the shaft once a week. If, after three weeks, nothing had changed, the mine could then be 'freed' by another miner – hence the origin of the slang word 'nicked'.

In addition to the Bull's Head in Monyash, Barmote Courts met at other pubs in the Peak District. Examples include the appropriately named Miner's Arms found in both Eyam and Brassington. In the mid

MINERS ARMS

Brassington was once a busy lead mining village, and the miners' special Barmote Court met at this well-known pub.

1800s, the landlord at the latter was a Thomas Slack, and he must have been quite a powerful man. Not only was he a publican but also the Barmaster of the Brassington Liberty (a 'liberty' was the district in which the miners searched for lead ore, and there were up to 50 in Derbyshire); and he sat with a jury of 24 men to rule on mining matters.

According to research by local historian Ron Slack, a detailed accounts book from this time still survives and shows just how central the pub was to community life. As the relatively wealthy landlord, Thomas Slack gave long credit and loans for various goods and services to the miners, and that of course included ale.

There is no doubt that after many long and demanding hours spent underground in fairly awful conditions, it would be quite normal to want to slake your thirst at the local pub or alehouse. But the Peak District miners' considerable need for liquids was also based on the fact that they believed ale protected them against lead poisoning. Whether the local landlord shared their belief is not known, but a man as astute as Thomas Slack would certainly have not tried to dissuade them.

As his namesake Ron Slack notes: "The characteristic entry in almost all the accounts held by miners is 'ale to mine' and he seems to have sold his ale whenever he carried out his official duties - 'ale at measuring' is a frequent entry, as is 'ale at gift' or 'ale at giving a mine'. This Barmaster prospered."

As landlord and Barmaster, he covered the fees for prospecting miners who hoped to go on and strike it lucky; but inevitably some ended up deep in debt, and these were often forced to help out at the landlord's bidding, doing odd jobs and helping at harvest time. Indeed, the records show that many of the miners practiced a dual economy and also farmed, and there are details of transactions involving animals and fodder.

Three Barmote Courts still meet today, although not in pubs, covering the Wirksworth, Chatsworth and Haddon Fields; but although they are technically still courts of law with judicial powers their role is mostly ceremonial. In simple administrative terms, your average Peak District ore field was split between major landowners such as the Duke of Devonshire and Duke of Rutland, but the Crown had a stake as well. Via the Duchy of Lancaster, it owned what's called the King's or Queen's Field – a term still kept alive in the name of the King's Field pub in Wirksworth.

The legacy of lead mining is remembered by the names of other pubs, and not just the Miner's Arms (which, in addition to Eyam and Brassington, is also represented at Carsington and Milltown, near Ashover). Until it closed in the mid 1990s, there was a hostelry in Via Gellia at the Bonsall turning called the Pig o'Lead.

A few miles away is the attractive village of Winster, another place rooted in the traditions of lead mining and where the Barmote Court once met at the Angel Inn, opposite the Market Hall. The pub is now a private house, but the lovely arched hall, which dates from the 1600s, has been preserved by the National Trust and is open to the public at certain times. Once the farmers used to trade their wares upstairs, while the miners would weigh their lead below.

At the head of Banktop, above the village, is the Miner's Standard pub, and like others of this name which used to exist in Bolehill (near Wirksworth) and

The Miner's Standard at Winster is named after the leadminers' measuring dish.

Bonsall, they were named after the so-called standard dish once used by the lead miners to measure their ore. It was usually a rectangular vessel which held around 15 pints, nine dishes making one load. The Winster pub dates from 1653, when it was originally built as a farmhouse. A century later it became an inn, thanks in no small measure to the increasing trade from the turnpike road from Grangemill.

However, a contrary view to the origin of its name is that it refers to the royal standard or flag of Charles II, raised at Nottingham and marking the start of the Civil War against Parliament. Derbyshire's lead miners rallied to the King's cause after he promised to cut the tithes payable on lead ore. Incidentally, there are a set of initials carved into the stone above the front door to the pub: EP EP FP. It's believed to refer to the original owners, who are either Edward, Elizabeth and son Francis, or Edith, Ella and their son Frank – depending on who you talk to. However, an alternative and far more entertaining version is that the initials stand for: 'Every person entering pays for a pint'.

Another Winster pub, long gone, is the Crown, which was located almost opposite Winster Hall and is now a private house. It was so cramped that they say that even sitting down you could still touch the ceiling! According to one story, miners used to meet at the pub in the evening to have a drink and compare samples of their best finds. Bits that dropped off were swept up and thrown into the fire when the land-lord cleared the tables, causing the flames to leap up in bright and colourful patterns.

One night a young man mischievously put a live firing cap on the table, and the publican not noticing what it was went to throw it into the fire with everything else. As he did so, other miners realised what it was and within seconds the pub emptied as people scrambled for the door. After the loud explosion, they all crept back in to find the landlord and his bar covered with a layer of soot. Apparently the landlord's wife was livid and refused to clear up the mess, forbidding her husband to come to bed until the pub was clean.

The overall decline of the lead mining industry in the Peak District was reflected in a change of name for a number of local pubs. The George Hotel at Youlgrave was formerly called the Pig of Lead (as well as the Church Hotel), while the ubiquitous Miner's Arms was often ditched for something more current or universal. Local examples include the Lathkil Hotel at Over Haddon and the Queen's Arms at Taddington – and see Chapter 7 for what happened at the latter when a new landlord suggested changing the name back again.

Food and drink

Side by side with liquid refreshment, pubs have always offered the weary traveller a bite to eat. In the past this might have been a hunk of bread and a lump of cheese, or a bowl of warming broth. The posher roadside inns, town taverns and hotels would no doubt have had some meat roasting, as the hungry and fatigued passengers alighting from the coaches stumbled towards the door. However, if some modern ploughman's lunches are anything to go by, lowly-paid farmhands could now also expect a neat roll and butter, a dollop of coleslaw and something green and fancy involving lettuce and peppers.

Today in the Peak District, catering continues to be an important factor in the economic viability of many pubs. Indeed, it has got to the stage where it is now uncommon to find a pub in the Peak District that *doesn't* serve food. Much to the chagrin of some conventional pub-goers, quite a few pubs in our region have become virtual restaurants, with tables numbered and laid for diners.

Traditional tap rooms or public bars have been absorbed into the main body of the pub, providing more table space for eaters; while some pubs have gone the whole hog (if you excuse the pun) and turned into actual restaurants. The Flouch Inn, for instance, on the edge of the moors north west of Sheffield, is (rather bizarrely) no longer a pub but a split Cantonese/Italian/Balti restaurant, while elsewhere some otherwise ordinary-looking local pubs are certainly not what they might seem.

The first is in New Mills, where the Beehive public house has had a curious history. The building was originally a toll house, hence the unusual, pointed design, but after the railway was built it was moved – lock, stock and all its barrels – to the present site on the junction of Albion Road.

You can still get a pint of real ale in its small and modern downstairs bar, but the traditional pub sign outside has been joined by another swing sign which reads 'Curry Stop'. If you look further there's a second that proclaims 'Taste of Bengal', since the bar is largely a holding area for the Indian restaurant upstairs.

A similar thing happened with the Board Inn at Whaley Bridge a few years ago, which the new owner turned into a Chinese restaurant in all but name (it's now reverted to being a pub once more). The Bull's Head, a large and historic, eighteenth-century inn at Old Glossop, is also run as half-pub, half-Indian restaurant/take-away. There are three dining rooms where it must be said that top-notch Indian food is served daily, but in addition the two small front bars are maintained for drinkers and casual visitors. Legend has it that a tunnel once linked the pub with the church opposite, allowing the monks to flee in times of difficulty, but I daresay that if they emerged today among the plates of lamb balti and chicken schazlik they would be in for a quite a surprise.

Some pubs, however, have been given over entirely to diners. The Grouse and Claret at Rowsley lost its small tap room in 2004, when owners Wolverhampton and Dudley knocked it through to create a vast, open-plan (and waitress-only) dining area. This was despite protests from the parish council who wanted it kept as a place where local people could chat over a drink (without having to eat), since apart from the posh hotels there are no other pubs left in the village.

Inevitably for somewhere as popular as the Peak District, national pub chains have muscled in, and although there are certain exceptions, it is unfortunately sometimes the case that (like the Grouse and Claret) when a long-established local inn is taken over it can turn into a rather bland dining pub furnished and run like every other in the same chain. For instance, the Highwayman at Eastmoor, on the A619 Baslow-Chesterfield road, is a perfectly friendly and well-run Brewsters pub, but if Dick Turpin turned up today he would no doubt be a little puzzled at the antics of a member of staff dressed up as a giant bear inviting his children to enjoy the 'Fun Factory'.

Food and drink is not surprisingly celebrated in the names of pubs in our region, although they are quite diverse. There's a Pineapple Inn on the High Street in New Mills, while the origin of the Baker's Arms on West Street in Buxton is fairly obvious. The Cheshire Cheese, just round the corner on the old High Street, is one of four such named pubs in the Peak District (see Chapter 2). You can get a Shoulder of Mutton at Bradwell and Chapel en le Frith, and season it with a trip to Ye Olde Mustard Pot at Midhopestones, between Langsett and Stocksbridge; then finish off with the Grapes on the Square at Longnor.

In addition to New Mills, there's another Beehive in the village of Combs, two miles west of Chapel-en-le-Frith; and as you would expect there are various references in pub names to the brewing trade itself. The Malt Shovel Inn at Wirksworth Moor, the Barrel Inn at Bretton (see Chapter 4) and the Jug and Glass on the A515 near the Hartington turning are all good examples; and both Ashbourne and Wirksworth boast pubs called the Vaults. At Marsden in West Yorkshire, on the extreme northern edge of the National Park, you can also find the Riverhead Brewery Tap, which as its name suggests brews its own beer. There are more details on this worthy establishment in Chapter 8.

The changing face of industry

Throughout the late eighteenth and nineteenth centuries as the Industrial Revolution took hold, new pubs were built to serve the growing workforce. Even in what we consider the relatively rural Peak District, there are plenty of public houses which date from this industrial period.

Don't forget that the Derwent Valley south of Matlock was in many ways the cradle of the Industrial Revolution, and a few years ago was internationally recognised with its designation as a World Heritage Site. It was here, in 1771, that Richard Arkwright built the world's first water-powered cotton spinning mill, and paved the way for mass production techniques that would usher in the modern factory system.

The small community of Cromford was largely established to house Arkwright's new workforce, and that included pubs, of course. The Greyhound Hotel, originally called the Black Greyhound (and known to locals as the Black Dog Inn), occupies a central position on the Market Place and was built in the late 1700s for the mill bosses and visiting businessmen. The hotel was also as a stopover on the Ashbourne to Chesterfield turnpike and for the regular coach to Manchester.

It's a grand and statesmanlike building, from its imposing Georgian entrance complete with pillars, through to the ornate clock at the top of the building, and was obviously built to impress. According to the local tale, the mill workers were not allowed inside the Greyhound, and instead were confined to one of the other pubs in Cromford. Chapter 8 details some of those that have now closed, including the Bull's Head, George and Dragon and Crown Inn, but one that has survived is the Boat Inn (out of sight around the corner from the Greyhound) that was almost certainly a watering hole for the masses. It was built in the 1770s, and was later known as the Hit and Miss – a reference to the varying quality of the beer, perhaps? The first landlord, a Mr Anthony Boden, was also a butcher, and the pub is described at a later auction as a brewhouse and slaughterhouse, giving a whole new meaning to the term 'getting slaughtered'.

Many of the older houses which line Cromford Hill, on the road up to Wirksworth, were also built by Arkwright to house his workforce, and in particular the well-preserved terraced rows on North Street, off the Hill. On opposite corners of this junction stood the Cock Inn and

Bell Inn. The former is now a private residence, but the Bell Inn, once known as the Blue Bell, remains open and is a fine example of a period public house (probably early nineteenth century), even retaining a traditional snug bar in the corner.

Another ostensibly rural location was also a focus of industrial activity. Bollington, on the north western side of the Peak District near Macclesfield, once boasted 13 cotton mills, but although production later switched to synthetic fibres, all the mills eventually closed. Luckily a couple have been preserved – Clarence (1841) and Adelphi (1856) – which now function as private apartments and offices.

With such a sizeable workforce, it was not surprising that the large village needed plenty of places for refreshment, and even today there as many as 19 pubs and clubs dotted around the place. The name of the Spinners Arms, on Palmerston Street, is a reminder of times past; and the Poachers Inn on Ingersley Road (formerly called the Masonic Inn) was converted about a century ago from several end-of-terrace mill-workers cottages.

Turnpikes and coaching inns

As we've seen in the previous chapter, the development of many of the early pubs in the Peak District was due to the needs of passing travellers, merchants, soldiers and pilgrims. In terms of transport, the packhorses weaved their way across the hills and moors with loads of salt, wool and ore, while other horse-drawn cargoes made their way slowly along rough and sometimes dangerous tracks.

The advent of turnpikes in the mid 1700s improved some journeys, but travel beyond your own patch was still a long and often difficult affair. The Wagon and Horses (Bollington), and the Coach and Horses (Ashbourne and Fenny Bentley) were among many roadside pubs and inns which offered stabling, and in some cases that could mean provision for dozens of horses.

Many of the larger pubs and inns that we use today were previously busy coaching inns. The Red Lion at Wirksworth is a handsome, eighteenth-century coaching and posting inn (as they were known) located on the Ashbourne turnpike. It offered generous stabling at the rear, as well as its own bowling green, and you can imagine a horse-drawn coach clip-clopping across the cobbles to emerge from under the tell-tale arch. Most if not all of those original stables from that era are now gone, with pubs converting them into garages and shops, or some-times into attractive accommodation (see the Castle Inn at Castleton, and the Crewe and Harpur Arms at Longnor).

Despite the poor condition of most roads, turnpikes did cut travelling times, and stagecoaches (and in particular mail coaches) demanded ever-speedier journeys. Passengers had to be fed immediately and horses changed at the double. In some cases, such as the all-important mail coaches, the turn-round time was as little as a minute or so, which required the main coaching inns to have considerable resources.

One example of a fine old coaching inn that continues to be a popular modern pub is the Ram's Head at Disley. Look out, in particular, for its surviving mounting steps out the front. Although in existence before the Manchester to Buxton turnpike came along in 1724 (the first turnpike in Derbyshire, in fact), it was in a fortunate position at the junction of several local routes. As late as 1860, the Manchester to Buxton Turnpike Trust was granted an Act of Parliament to sort out its financial affairs, but by then the viability of turnpikes was almost at an end.

Further along the route, at Buxton, two of the most established coaching inns were said to have worked out a mutually beneficial system, with traffic on the Manchester to London route shared by the town's main coaching inns – the Eagle and Child, and the White Hart. On the southbound journey passengers breakfasted at the White Hart, while on the return journey they enjoyed evening dinner at the Eagle.

Another coaching inn which benefited from the coaching trade was the Newhaven House Hotel, built in 1795 by the 5th Duke of Devonshire at the meeting point of important new turnpikes from Derby and Nottingham on what is now the A515. It was originally called the Devonshire Arms until, it seems, the land became part of the Duke of Rutland's estate in the nineteenth century.

Writing in 1905, J. B. Firth described his impressions:

Such an inn was badly needed, for previously there had been only a few mean little houses of call between Ashbourne and Buxton, and travellers were grateful to the Duke of Devonshire for this roadside palace which he built for their comfort. It now looks ghostly and deserted... but it used to have every bedroom occupied every night, and was as gay and fashionable as a London hotel.

Today Newhaven still remains little more than a hamlet, as isolated and remote as it was a century ago, and for most car drivers just a blur as they journey between Ashbourne and Buxton, or emerge on the A5012 from Cromford. But once this was a meeting point for travellers, farmers and merchants from Nottinghamshire, Derbyshire, Stafford-

Built in 1795, the Newhaven House Hotel was once an important coaching inn on the Derby to Buxton turnpike, but has been closed for some years.

shire and Cheshire, and until the early twentieth century it was the venue for an annual fair held at the end of October that attracted huge numbers of people buying and selling all manner of goods, including sheep and cattle.

It its heyday, the Newhaven House Hotel was described by one visitor as "a large handsome and commodious inn, where travellers meet with every requisite accommodation, including stabling for 100 horses." A story connected with the inn, almost certainly apocryphal, is that George IV once stayed there while on his royal travels, and so delighted was he with the hospitality he received that he granted the inn a free and perpetual licence.

Regardless of this, the hotel closed a number of years ago, since when it has remained in a semi-derelict state on the verge, you hope, of making a comeback. Mind you, it's not the only pub on this stretch of road to have struggled against adversity. A mile to the north the Jug and Glass opened in the early 1800s, in effect acting as the alehouse to the hotel at Newhaven. In the 1990s it was completely gutted by fire, and although rebuilt today only opens seasonally.

Other imposing coaching inns include the George Hotel at Tideswell, the Ashford Arms at Ashford in the Water, the Wheatsheaf at Baslow and the George Hotel at Hathersage. The last is today a plush Best Western hotel catering for the upper end of the market, but in its time was a popular stopping place for passengers en route from Castleton to Sheffield – a journey which now takes under an hour but 250 years ago took eight times as long.

The Derwent Hotel at Whatstandwell, by the bridge over the River Derwent between Cromford and Ambergate, was also a key location for stagecoaches. Not only was it on the Derby to Manchester route, but it was also where coachmen would prepare their horses for the steep ascent to Crich.

Chapel en le Frith was evidently important for travellers venturing east across the moors of the Peak District, with stagecoaches and wagons regularly setting off from its busy market place. Dotted around this hive of activity were, at one time, four separate pubs, with more along Market Street.

Canals and railways

The days of turnpikes and universal coach travel were cut short by the advent of industrialisation, which ushered in a transport revolution. Eventually they were eclipsed by the railways, of course, but initially the competition (at least, as far as long-haul freight traffic was concerned) was from the new canal network.

The topography of the Peak District didn't necessarily suit either canals or railways, but that didn't stop the engineers from trying. The Cromford Canal linked the Derwent Valley with the national canal network to the south, while the Peak Forest Canal did the same in the north west at Whaley Bridge. The wharf, at the northern end of the town, is still popular with narrow boats, and is a busy and colourful place. On nearby Johnson Street is the Navigation Inn, a pleasant mid eighteenth-century pub which still caters for visiting water-borne trade.

Pubs like this flourished with the labour-intensive construction of the canals (and later the railways), a point echoed at the Dog and Partridge a little further down Buxton Road. Located within a few yards of the canal, it was built to satisfy the considerable thirst of the navvies, although, like Cromford, this smart and attractive pub tended to be for the managers, while the rank and file headed for the beer house which was once located through the archway a few properties away.

The Dog and Partridge sits beside the short, Whaley Bridge arm of

One of the Peak District's few canal pubs is the Navigation Inn at Buxworth, at the terminus of the Peak Forest Canal near Whaley Bridge.

the canal, which after it connects to the main waterway goes on to join the Macclesfield Canal. However, the Peak Forest Canal continues another mile or so eastwards to Buxworth, where the old canal basin remains Britain's only canal-tramway interchange.

Quarried limestone from Dove Holes was brought down a gravity-fed tramway six and a half miles long and loaded on to the waiting boats at Buxworth Basin. Teams of five horses then pulled the empty wagons back up the incline plane. On the downward journey a boy called a 'nipper' was employed to brake the leading wagon by thrusting a wooden rod into the wheel spokes. The tramway was initially single-track, but soon was converted to double, apart for a short section of tunnel.

The construction of the tramway was authorised by an Act of Parliament in 1794, and building work was largely completed by 1799. Throughout the next century the canal and tramway provided an important source of employment and commercial activity, with local paper and cotton mills also benefiting from the new access. Such was the level of business that Buxworth was at one time described as "a thriving inland canal port". By the turn of the twentieth century, the fortunes of both canal and tramway were ebbing, and by the 1920s they fell into disuse. However, there are plans to renovate the historic canal basin, a scheduled ancient monument, and make Buxworth navigable once more.

Next to the basin, where the horses from the Peak Forest Tramway would be marshalled and the stone prepared for loading, is the Navigation Inn (yes, another!). This long and handsome brick-built building was constructed over 200 years ago and is stuffed full of canal memorabilia. Prints, books, rope knots, tea towels – you name it, if it's got anything to do with canals, you will probably find it in this pub. Another claim to fame is that it was once owned by Pat Phoenix, *Coronation Street's* Elsie Tanner.

One other interesting story connected with this intriguing place concerns its name. You might notice that the interpretation boards on the canal-side refer to 'Bugsworth' Basin, but the road signs spell the name 'Buxworth'. In 1929, the local headmaster and vicar jointly led a successful campaign to gentrify the name from the traditional 'Bugsworth' to the apparently more palatable 'Buxworth'.

The name originally came from the Buggesworth family, who moved here from Nottinghamshire in the Middle Ages, and in Old English it literally means 'Bugge's enclosure.' Since the change in 1929, there have been a number of attempts to switch it back, and in 1949 someone rather cheekily suggested changing it altogether to 'Mugsworth' since they had been foolish to alter such an historic name in the first place. The latest attempt to restore 'Bugsworth' was defeated by three to two in a local vote in 1999. So, to most it is 'Buxworth', but to others it will always be 'Buggie'.

Another former canal pub is located on the Huddersfield Narrow Canal near Marsden in West Yorkshire. Now called the Water's Edge Restaurant and a licensed café rather than a pub, it stands by the entrance to the recently re-opened Standedge Tunnel. Today the Tunnel End Inn (formerly the Junction Inn) on nearby Waters Road is probably the nearest bona fide pub.

Thomas Telford's tunnel below the Pennines was hewn out of solid rock at the turn of the eighteenth century and today is the longest (3.75 miles), deepest (638ft underground) and also the highest (645ft above sea level) navigable canal tunnel in Britain. Organised trips explore the subterranean waterway during the summer, and it's a fascinating, if rather chilly, experience. A former transhipment warehouse on the quayside near Marsden has also been restored, and now houses a visitor centre with a range of interactive displays and exhibitions.

The tunnel emerges on the western side of the Pennines at Diggle, where the Diggle Hotel at the hamlet of Digglea served as an alehouse and stores for the navvies employed to dig the tunnel. Before that it was a weaver's cottage, with the mill and looms on the top floor. Now that the tunnel has been reopened the management at the Diggle Hotel say that they are busier than ever – it's uncanny how these things have a habit of going full circle. Some of the spoil from the navvies' backbreaking work was dumped on the bare moorland above, including piles that can still be seen near the Great Western pub on the A62 high above Marsden.

Other pubs from this time reflect the changing face of transport, and as is often the case you can tell a lot through their actual names. In general, most coaching inns didn't specifically take a related name (such as the Coach and Horses), since the pubs themselves were refreshment points or overnight stops and so were integral to travel by stagecoach.

But when the railways came along in the mid 1800s, publicans realised that their establishments were no longer involved in the actual running of this new form of mass transport - there were separate stations, of course. So when a new railway line was built it was common for pubs which considered themselves in the vicinity to change their name in an attempt to attract new customers. Hence the rash of Railway Hotels or Station Taverns, even though some of them weren't always particularly close to a line. Today there are still over 400 pubs in the UK with 'railway' in their name.

The Midland railway company forged an ambitious new route through the middle of the Peak District, via Matlock and Bakewell, and although it was not without its problems and setbacks, it inevitably provided new opportunities for pubs and inns. The names of two current pubs by the road bridge at Matlock Bath – the County and Station, and the Midland – remember this early period; and further up the line the origin of the Railway Inn at Matlock is also self-explanatory.

A few miles north along the Derwent valley at Rowsley, what is now the Grouse and Claret used to be called the Station Hotel. Nearby was a large marshalling yard complete with engine shed, while Rowsley Station was often busy with visitors alighting for Chatsworth House (the original station building designed by Sir Joseph Paxton is now marooned in the middle of the newly-built Peak Shopping Village development). The railway didn't continue up the Derwent to Chatsworth because the Duke of Devonshire refused to let the line through his grounds; so instead the railway veered sharply west along the edge of the Wye valley and via a tunnel beneath Haddon Hall (a hard-won compromise with the Duke of Rutland) to Bakewell.

The railway brought new custom to the market town on the River Wye, even though the station was not exactly in the centre, and not surprisingly a Station Hotel soon appeared; but further up the line the Monsal Head Hotel profited considerably from the new trade.

This was originally a two-storey, traditional whitewashed stone pub called the Bull's Head, but when the modern tourist industry began to find its feet the pub was completely rebuilt some time around the 1880s and renamed the Station Hotel. Guests were met at the halt in the dale bottom below and brought up to the hotel by horse and carriage. All that's left from the original pub is a stone relief of a bull's head, incorporated above the main entrance; otherwise the rather ostentatious, three-storey building bears little resemblance to what went before – nor, with its almost Alpine wooden frontage, does it have much in common with any other building at Monsal Head.

That said, it's a popular place today, with a reputation for good food and a decent choice of real ale (including the specially-brewed Monsal Bitter), and the views down to the famous railway viaduct and along Monsal Dale are sublime. All that's missing now is the actual railway. For more details on the Stables Bar next door see the previous chapter.

Beyond Monsal Head, the line negotiated more tunnels, viaducts and cuttings before arriving at Miller's Dale, where apart from the limestone quarries there was a connection for a branch line service to Buxton. The station, which had three platforms, was also unusual in having its own post office. Nearby was the Railway Hotel, which later changed its name to the Dale Hotel. With the closure of the line and station in 1967, the hotel soon followed suit, and now forms two private dwellings.

Originally a traditional cottage pub called the Bull's Head, the Monsal Head Hotel was rebuilt and renamed in the 1880s to cater for the visitors brought in by the new railway.

Further to the north, trade at the Stanhope Arms at Dunford Bridge, South Yorkshire, was given a boost with the construction of the railway across the Pennines. This was the famous route up the Longdendale valley via Crowden and Woodhead, and until the first tunnel was built, passengers transferred to coaches for the journey across the bleak central moorland section.

Over a thousand thirsty navvies were employed to dig the tunnels and lay the route, living in temporary accommodation at the head of Longdendale. How the Stanhope Arms and all the other pubs at these remote rural locations must have profited.

Two pubs in particular, high on the moors by the turning off the A628 to Dunford Bridge, did particularly well out of the huge influx of itinerant workers. The Plough and Harrow was located at the actual summit, a place sometimes known as Fiddlers Green, while its rival was the Millers Arms, which could be found just across the bleak moorland at the now long-vanished community at Saltersbrook. However, once the tunnels had been dug, and the dams for the new reservoirs constructed, the inns and alehouses soon died away – see Chapter 8 on the lost pubs of Crowden and Woodhead.

Passenger services ended in 1970 and the railway was finally scrapped in 1981, since when the main road (A628) has provided a key route for travellers between Manchester and Sheffield. However, with the exception of the tunnels, much of the former railway trackbed has been converted to the Trans Pennine Trail, a coast-to-coast route for walkers, cyclists and horse riders which links Southport and Liverpool with Hull and Hornsea, a distance of 213 miles (344km). One beneficial result for certain pub goers is that you can now leave your horse in a purpose-built area for horses and their boxes close to the Stanhope Arms.

There's also a Railway Inn at Whaley Bridge, near the station as you would expect; and further along the line, at Furness Vale, a pub called the Crossings is appropriately next to the level crossing by Furness Vale station. Across the valley, at New Mills, the North Western is handily-placed for Newtown Station, with its sign depicting a steam train in full flight.

The Railway Hotel near Hurdlow, a hamlet off the A515 north of Hartington, was originally a farmstead, but took advantage of the opportunities presented by the new Cromford and High Peak line built between 1825-30 across the high limestone uplands; and then later the Ashbourne-Buxton line which joined the former near Hurdlow at Parsley Hay.

Both lines were closed by 1967, but thanks to the Peak District National Park and Derbyshire County Council, reopened a few years later as traffic-free recreational routes for walkers, cyclists and horseriders. Since then, the Railway Hotel has been renamed the Royal Oak and especially during the summer, the pub is busy with walkers and cyclists. There's even a bunkhouse and camping field to the rear.

These two off-road routes – the High Peak and Tissington Trails – are particularly popular given the state of many of today's main roads. The modern highway changed irrevocably with the advent of the motor car, and on a busy summer's weekend the Peak District echoes to the sight, sound and sometimes smell of large numbers of cars, coaches, caravans and motorbikes.

Instead of providing for wagons and horse-drawn coaches, modern pubs have wide strips of tarmac for lines of cars, and some (like the Bluebell Inn on the A515 near Tissington) even have designated bays for coach parking. A few decades ago it was not unusual for so-called road-house pubs to offer their car-driving customers a complete service.

The Red Lion at Wirksworth, previously cited as an example of a coaching inn, also offered a motor garage; and in my own village of Youlgrave, people remember the sight of petrol pumps outside the Bull's Head and Farmyard Inn. The famous gallows sign belonging to the Green Man and Black's Head Royal Hotel in Ashbourne, which stretches across the street, used to have boards either side of the central picture reading 'garage' and 'petrol'. Now most local people go the nearby supermarket to fill up with diesel and unleaded – perhaps we are moving backwards, after all?

4

People and Places

Lords and Ladies

On a national level, the most common pub names are connected with the church and monarchy (see Chapter 7), but locally they also reflect an allegiance to or ownership by the Lord of the Manor.

In the case of the Peak District one of the names which regularly crops up is the Devonshire Arms, named after the Cavendish family of Chatsworth. It is hardly surprising that the name is so popular, given that the Duke of Devonshire owns large tracts of the surrounding land (including the pubs) and through one means or another he employed plenty of local people.

Inevitably most of the Devonshire Arms are to be found in the centre of the Peak District in and around his main estate. Bakewell, Baslow, Beeley, Buxton, Pilsley and Sheldon all have Devonshire Arms, and there are others at Hartington and Buxton. I understand that the Duke William on Church Street, Matlock – a listed building dating from the 1750s – was also once a manor house belonging to the Duke of Devonshire (hence its name).

Until only a few years ago, the Ashford Arms at Ashford in the Water also used to be called the Devonshire Arms (and before that the Stags Head); while the Devonshire Arms at Peak Forest is also named after the family, but along with much else in the village was sold by auction in 1954 to pay the 10th Duke's death duties.

However, the connections with the Cavendishes are not severed quite that easily. Opposite the pub is the parish church, which unusually is dedicated to 'Charles, King and Martyr'. The original church was built in 1657 by the Countess of Devonshire, an ardent Royalist, after her favourite son was killed by Parliamentarians while fighting for Charles I fourteen years earlier. The present church dates from 1877 and was built by the 7th Duke of Devonshire. Previous ministers included an enterprising chap who granted on-the-spot marriage licenses to eloping couples, and for a while Peak Forest had the reputation as the Gretna Green of the Peak.

A little further west along the A623 at Sparrowpit, another

Devonshire Arms changed its name to the Wanted Inn in the 1950s; while one of the Duke's most famous racehorses, the Flying Childers, is commemorated in the name of the village pub at Stanton in Peak (see Chapter 7 for the full story of these two unusually-named pubs).

The family is also identified with the Cavendish Hotel at Baslow, which paradoxically was originally owned by the Duke of Rutland and called the Peacock. The hotel was bought by the Duke of Devonshire in 1830, and rebuilt in the early 1970s. The sign for the Cavendish Hotel depicts a snake, which is part of the family's coat of arms. This, in turn, explains the name of one of the Peak District's most famous roads, and with it another pub.

The Snake Pass Inn stands beside the modern A57, about four miles from the western end of the Ladybower Reservoir, and was built in 1821 following the opening of the major east-west road over the high and inhospitable moorland of Bleaklow. The new route across the Dark Peak, plotted by Thomas Telford, linked Sheffield to Glossop and Manchester. It rises to 1,680ft (512m) at its summit, where the Pennine Way National Trail crosses on its lonely way from Kinder Scout to Bleaklow, and today the road is still regularly cut off in bad weather each winter.

The inn, which was originally called Lady Clough House after the clough or valley above which it stands, is not named after the tortuous

The elegant Peacock Hotel at Rowsley was built in 1652 by the Manners family of Haddon Hall, and takes its name from the bird that adorns the Duke of Rutland's coat of arms.

and looping course of the road as many suspect, but after the snake which features on the Duke of Devonshire's crest as displayed at the Baslow hotel. It was he that petitioned for the route and engaged the services of Telford.

There are plenty of other, famous local families rooted in the Peak District. The Manners of Haddon Hall are still important ducal landowners, with the Duke of Rutland remembered by a pub bearing his name at Baslow. It was originally called the Green Man, according to the present landlord, who also repeats the well-known story of the secret tunnel that supposedly runs from the pub to Chatsworth. Why the two should be connected is anyone's guess.

The well-known Rutland Arms Hotel dominates Rutland Square in the centre of Bakewell (see Chapter 6), and further down Haddon Road you can also find the Manners Hotel. The Duke's crest features a peacock, which is why there are Peacock Hotels at Bakewell and Rowsley, as well as others on the edge of the Peak at Cutthorpe and Owler Bar.

The Peacock Hotel at Rowsley is particularly interesting, since it was built in 1652 as the private residence for John Stevenson, agent to the Manners family. After briefly becoming the dower house and later a farm, it was converted into a hotel in the 1820s, at the same time as the closure of Rowsley's two coaching and posting inns on the Square (the Nag's Head and Red Lion).

The elegant, ivy-clad building has had its fair share of distinguished and unusual guests, including the poet Henry Wadsworth Longfellow, and Maximillian, the nineteenth-century Emperor of Mexico. Today the stylish dining room and atmospheric Peacock Bar, with its beamed ceiling and ornately carved wooden bar, still exude elegance, and it remains one of the very few pubs/hotels in the Peak which is licensed to hold weddings.

Of course, landowners like the Dukes of Devonshire and Rutland owned other pubs in the Peak District whose name bore no obvious connection with their families. We've already seen how the Duke of Rutland once used the Fox House Inn as overspill accommodation for his shooting parties, while further down the road towards Froggatt, he also owned the Chequers Inn. The Duke used this eighteenth-century coaching inn to collect rent from his local tenants, but it was said that after he had gathered it up he would treat them all to food and ale at the pub.

Another powerful local family were the Eyres, most closely associated with Hassop, Calver and Hathersage. The sign for the Eyre Arms at Hassop shows the family coat of arms, the centrepiece of which is a solitary leg.

The story behind this curious design apparently goes all the way back to an incident involving William the Conqueror at the Battle of Hastings in 1066. Knocked from his horse during the fighting, the King was helped by a soldier who loosened the King's helmet. William asked the fellow for his name (it was, rather improbably, Truelove) to which the King said: "I shall call you Air, for you have given me air to breathe." Later in the same battle the King discovered that Truelove (or Air) had been injured, and had to have a leg amputated (hence the unusual family crest). William told him that when he was sufficiently recovered he would give

The Eyre's family crest, depicted in the sign for the Eyre Arms at Hassop, includes a solitary leg.

him some land – to which the grateful soldier replied: "I shall call it Hope, for you have given me hope to live."

Despite the rather fanciful tale, the Eyres went on to own a considerable amount of land and a number of properties, such as Nether Hall in the Hope Valley and North Lees Hall above Hathersage, although the ancestral home until the 1850s was Hassop Hall. Today it's privately owned and run as an exclusive restaurant.

Nearby is the seventeenth-century Eyre Arms, a handsome, creeper-covered building with a lovely walled garden to the side. The traditional interior has been well-maintained and remains full of character, especially when the open fires are roaring on a chilly winter's night. Apart from the resident ghost (see Chapter 5), the most eye-catching feature is the massive coat of arms on the wall of the lounge bar, which belongs to Rowland Eyre, a Royalist officer in the Civil War. The Eyres were fervent Roman Catholics and diehard supporters of the King, and Rowland Eyre raised a regiment in Derbyshire and fought for the Crown at the Battle of Marston Moor in 1644.

Another pub with connections to the Eyre family is the Derwentwater Arms at nearby Calver. It used to be called the

Newburgh Arms, since the Earldom of Newburgh was one of the Eyre family titles. In fact, the Eyre Arms at Hassop was also called the Newburgh Arms until 1902. There was also once another Newburgh Arms in Bradwell, but it is now a private house.

The Duke of Norfolk (the Howards) also owned considerable tracts of land around the fringes of the Peak District, especially in the vicinity of Sheffield and Glossop, and as late as 1924 the Howards still retained the title of Lords of the Manor of Glossop. Indeed, the Duke was instrumental in the development of the modern mill town, which was originally known as Howardstown, and it's no surprise that there's a Norfolk Arms on Norfolk Square in the centre of Glossop, and two further pubs of this name on the moors above Sheffield at Ringinglow and Rivelin (as well as others in the city centre and at Handsworth, Grenoside and Chapeltown).

The Earldom of Surrey was another title that belonged to the Howards, which explains why there was once a Surrey Arms off the A57 towards Moscar Top west of Sheffield, as well as two more in Glossop: the one on Victoria Street was known by locals as 'Top Surrey' and the other on High Street West was called 'Bottom Surrey'. The family's coat of arms features a white lion, which of course has itself become a fairly common pub name these days.

The Crewe and Harpur Arms at Longnor, a handsome brick-built country inn on the main square, is named after the family behind Calke Abbey. Calke, now run by the National Trust, remains little-changed since it was built 300 years ago for the reclusive Harpurs (later the Harpur-Crewes). The family once owned several other pubs in the central/south Peak, including the Traveller's Rest at Flash Bar.

Meanwhile, the Earls of Derby are remembered by the Stanley Arms, located in a remote valley bottom off the Buxton to Macclesfield road at a location known as Bottom-of-the-Oven. The unusual name is thought to come from a large oven or spit roast that was once a feature of nearby Oven Lane, and which fed the men of Lord Stanley of Crag Hall (at nearby Wildboarclough, and still the family's summer home).

Former pubs at Gradbach and Buxton, both called the Eagle and Child, referred to the Stanley's family coat of arms. Their main seat is at Knowsley, near Liverpool, where their family crest is known as the 'bird and babby'. The story behind the unusual design - according, once more, to popular tradition – dates back to the 1300s when, unbeknown to his wife, the Earl of Derby had an illegitimate son. He hid the baby in an eagle's nest on his land, and then when out his with his wife they 'discovered' the child, which he claimed must have been taken by an eagle. They subsequently adopted the child, hence the family's unusual coat of arms. You can still see the simple engraving and inscription above the door of the former roadside pub at Gradbach, which was open between 1738 and 1919.

Another unique family name is celebrated by the Woodroffe Arms in the village of Hope, near Castleton. The Woodroffes (or Woodroofes) were once the official King's Foresters of the Peak, acting as forest officers to supervise the royal hunting ground which once spread across much of the High Peak. According to a fascinating booklet by the Hope Historical Society, the Woodroffes pre-eminence dates back to the mid 1400s, when they distinguished themselves fighting for Edward IV and were granted the right to bear arms. The family motto reads: *Quod transtuli restuli*, or 'That which I took out I brought back'. In the past, family members have been innkeepers at the pub; and the position of Hope Parish Clerk was, until 1855, passed down from father to son for over 200 consecutive years.

The Maynard Arms at Grindleford was built in 1908, and its imposing countenance, as well as its roadside location just to the north of the village near the turning for the station, reflects the importance which the railway played in bringing visitors into the area. The Totley Tunnel, which begins just after Grindleford station and takes the Sheffield-bound trains deep under the moors, was dug in the 1890s and at 6,230 yards (5,694m) is one of the longest railway tunnels in Britain.

The Maynards, incidentally, have an impressive family pedigree, although their connection with the Peak District only goes back to the 1800s when Anthony Maynard acquired land, including the Manor of Nether Padley. Sir Richard Maynard fought for King Henry V at Agincourt in 1415; then a century later Thomas Maynard helped defeat the Scots at Flodden Field. The family coat of arms is displayed on the hotel sign.

Meanwhile, moving much further down the Derwent valley to Ambergate, south of Cromford, the Hurt Arms is named after a notable Derbyshire family whose seat has traditionally been at nearby Alderwasley. After the pub was refurbished in the mid 1990s the owners decided to change its name, but such was local resistance to the plan (residents even staged a protest meeting) that the idea was quickly dropped and the Hurt Arms it remains.

The Okeover Arms at Mappleton on the River Dove north of Ashbourne remembers the local Okeover family, who have lived at the hall since Norman times. Both the hall and church were plundered by the Jacobites of Bonnie Prince Charlie's army as they swept through here in 1745.

Another noteworthy Peak District family is remembered in the name of the Jodrell Arms Hotel by the railway station at Whaley Bridge. It's named in honour of the Jodrells who were major landowners in these parts from the thirteenth century, and whose fortunes took a sharp upward turn after William Jodrell distinguished himself as an archer at the Battle of Crecy in 1346. He established the family home at Yeardsley Hall, and the estate grew to include Shallcross Hall near Taxal.

The present Jodrell Arms at Whaley Bridge replaced an earlier building thought to date from the 1690s. Among the major alterations in the nineteenth century was an elaborate Tuscan porch on its west side, constructed so that the building would face west towards the passengers alighting at the new railway station. The family is also remembered by the rather more modern Jodrell Bank radio telescope on the Cheshire Plain.

Peak personalities

There are plenty of interesting and distinguished people who have associations with the pubs, inns and hotels of the Peak District, and one of the best known of the historical figures is Mary, Queen of Scots.

During her captivity she was held at Chatsworth, from where she was taken on four occasions to Buxton in the hope that the health-giving spa water would improve her poor health. Her custodian at Chatsworth was the 6th Earl of Shrewsbury, fourth husband of the famous Bess of Hardwick, and it was at his hotel in Buxton that the doomed Scottish queen stayed.

Her confinement at the Old Hall Hotel was carefully ordered, and followed the strict instructions of Queen Elizabeth. Mary was required to give one hour's notice if she wanted to leave her rooms, and she was not allowed any guests after 9pm. Strangers to the town were quizzed or even prevented from entering when Mary was resident at the hotel. There was also a rumour – and only a rumour – that Elizabeth intended to journey north and visit the hotel in disguise to see for herself her troublesome young cousin Mary.

Despite the curbs on her freedom, Mary apparently enjoyed her visits, and looked forward to her trips to the spa town. It is said that on her last visit to the hotel, in 1584, Mary scratched a message on the window of her bedroom with her diamond ring: "Buxton whose warm waters have made thy name famous, perchance, I shall visit thee no more, farewell!"

The Earl of Shrewsbury's hotel, built in the 1570s, is thought to have replaced an older inn on the same site with the same name but spelled 'Auld Hall'. The present building mostly dates from the time of the Duke of Devonshire's renovations in 1670, and it was always believed that most of the original building had been demolished. However, careful investigation has shown that the original structure is still in place behind the newer façade.

Either way, it remains a handsome old building located opposite the Pavilion Gardens at the end of the Crescent. A tiny bar at the end of the hotel is popular with visitors to performances at the Opera House across the road, offering pre- and post-theatre evening supper, and a special side door opens for just that purpose. The elegant Opera House, designed by Frank Matcham and opened in 1905, has undergone recent extensive renovation and is once more resplendent with its interior furnishings of gold leaf and velvet. It holds a variety of performances throughout the year, including the annual Buxton Music Festival.

Royal and military figures, many of whom have given their name to a pub, are covered in Chapter 7, but on top of this there are other notable characters and personalities who are remembered by the names of Peak District inns.

Charles Cotton and Izaak Walton are two of the most well-known literary figures, famous as the seventeenth-century authors of *The Compleat Angler*. This reflective treatise on fly fishing in the Peak District has been reprinted innumerable times, and although the authors praise a number of rivers the one that is most closely associated with the two philosophical anglers is the River Dove. The Izaak Walton Hotel at Ilam and the Charles Cotton Hotel at Hartington celebrate this pair, although the latter was formerly known as the Sleigh Arms after a local family.

However, all is not so clear-cut at Grindleford, where there is some measure of confusion over the true identity of the person after which the Sir William Hotel is named. On the face of it the public house (which was originally called the Bluebell, and then the Commercial Inn) appears to take its name from the well-known Sir William Hill Road. This runs directly westwards up the hillside from Grindleford towards the 1,407ft (427m) Sir William Hill summit, and then on to Eyam and Hucklow Edge and the Barrel Inn at Bretton. It should be pointed out that the Sir William Hill Road proved to be so testing for horse-drawn traffic that an easier route was created via Eyam – the B6521, also called

New Road – but recent landslips have in turn caused problems with this route.

So much for the name, but *who* does it actually refer to? There are, rather confusingly, a large number of candidates – a real posse of Sir Williams, as it were. An early suggestion, put forward by guidebook writer M. Baddeley in 1899, is that the hill might have been named after Sir William Peveril, illegitimate son of William the Conqueror. He was certainly a big cheese in this area in Norman times, and of course left us Peveril Castle in nearby Castleton, but it's not clear if he was ever knighted.

Then, moving on a few centuries through local history, there's Sir William Cavendish of the Chatsworth line – all four of them, in fact. They kicked off with Sir William Cavendish, Bess of Hardwick's

The identity of the Sir William after which this pub at Grindleford is named remains something of a mystery, since there are several contenders.

second husband (1505-1557), who was followed by their son Sir William (the 1st Earl of Devonshire) and so on.

As influential as the Cavendish family have been and to some extent still are in the Peak District, these Sir Williams are probably not front runners when it comes to having a pub in Grindleford named after them. A far better proposition is Sir William Saville, who was the 2nd Marquis of Halifax and Lord of the Manor of Eyam, and whose family had been given the Derbyshire parish by his relative Mary, Countess of Pembroke, in 1616. Sir William commanded Royalist forces during the Civil War, occupying Leeds and Wakefield, but being denied Bradford by the Roundheads under Fairfax. He became Governor of Sheffield and was killed in Yorkshire in 1644.

Over a century later came another strong contender for the pub title – Sir William Bagshawe, local landowner and country gentleman. He inherited his Derbyshire estate at the age of 30, and in a long and productive life raised 23 children (of whom 19 survived), was a respected physician and patron of the arts, and ultimately was appointed High

Sheriff of Derbyshire. Sir William held land at Oakes Park at Norton near Sheffield, Goosehill Hall at Castleton, and Wormhill Hall near Miller's Dale, and it is he who is *supposed* to have constructed the eponymous road across the hill in order to link his estates.

Perhaps bearing in mind this, plus the hill, then the last Sir William would seem the most likely candidate in terms of also having the pub named after him; but if you ask behind the bar they tend to favour Sir William Saville. To bolster their case they reproduce this sad entry from the Eyam Parish Register of February 4, 1692: "Elizabeth, wife of John Trout, she dyed upon the moor near unto Sir William a place so called, coming from Tideswell market in the snow." On this basis, Sir William Bagshaw, who wasn't born until 1771, came along 80 years too late.

I turned to the local Women's Institute, that bastion of common sense, for some help, but in their otherwise excellent booklet guide to the village, they sit firmly on the fence when it comes to the origin of the pub name. Mind you, they do confirm that the Sir William Hotel used to be called the Commercial Inn, as it still is by some older residents, and only gained its present name in 1925. Perhaps those wise locals are steering the best course?

A local character we do know more about, and of whom there was (I think) just the one, was Jesse Watts Russell. His name lives on at the Watts Russell Inn at Hopedale, an out-of-the-way hamlet tucked away in a narrow valley south of Alstonefield near Hartington. This wealthy, nine-teenth-century industrial magnate lived at nearby Ilam Hall, and was responsible for redesigning the estate village as well as the hall and church. The angular peaks of Dove Dale were said to remind him of the Alps, so he had the new buildings follow a mock-Gothic, Alpine theme. What's left of the hall is now a Youth Hostel, and the estate is managed by the National Trust.

Industrial magnate Jesse Watts Russell built Ilam Hall and is remembered by this pub at nearby Hopedale.

Someone else who was active in industry was Joseph Whitworth

(1803-87), who although born in Stockport, spent the last 15 years of his life at Stancliffe Hall in the Derwent Valley north of Matlock. He was a gifted mechanical engineer and inventor of the standard screw thread, but he also made a name for himself in armaments and is remembered by the Whitworth rifle. Like other Victorian industrialists, Whitworth also had a strong philanthropic streak, and founded a complex of public buildings centred on the Joseph Whitworth Institute which still stands in Darley Dale by the side of the A6. Adjoining the main centre is a recently renovated hotel (Grade II listed) that dates from the same period, and where you can enjoy a leisurely pint and a meal in pleasant surroundings.

I don't suppose Florence Nightingale was ever much of a pub-goer, but she spent much of her early life in Derbyshire, centred on the village of Lea above the Derwent valley south of Matlock. The family home was Lea Hurst, which is now, rather appropriately, a nursing home. The 'Lady with the Lamp' made her name tending wounded soldiers in the Crimea, of course, but later on she returned to Derbyshire in an attempt to shun the publicity that had enveloped her.

The pleasant village pub at Lea, the Jug and Glass, is closely associated with her family, if not Florence herself. It was part of a row of weavers' cottages built in 1782 by landowner Peter Nightingale (Florence's uncle) for use as a health centre or makeshift hospital for his estate workers. Following its conversion to a pub, the building was used for annual rent collection on so-called 'Nightingale Rent Days'. After collecting all the money and receiving the usual comments and complaints, the day would traditionally end with the landlord serving everyone a complimentary meal.

Folk heroes

Although Nottinghamshire lies outside the edge of the Peak District, the legendary outlaw Robin Hood is remembered in the names of several pubs in our region. The first is at Buxton on the Ashbourne Road, a second on Smithy Lane in Rainow, and the third on the Baslow-Chesterfield road (A619) east of Baslow – a location now simply known as Robin Hood. Apart from the nearby Robin Hood Farm, there's not much else there apart from the pub. It's thought that an inn of some sort has stood either here or near here since the late 1600s, as it's on one of the main eastbound routes out of the central Peak District. The Duke of Rutland once owned the buildings and surrounding land, but in 1920 it was sold to the Chesterfield Brewery, who in turn were taken over by

Mansfield Brewery in 1935.

In the last few decades the pub has become an increasingly popular destination for weekend walkers and climbers, so much so that in 1974 the landlord opened an uncarpeted bar called the Hiker's Den, where muddy boots and dogs are welcome. The main attraction for outdoor types is the eye-catching gritstone outcrop of Birchen Edge, which rises amid the bracken and heather behind the pub, towards the far end of which is Nelson's Monument. This commemorates the Battle of Trafalgar, and for good measure the three prominent tors on top of the edge are known as the Three Ships and inscribed with the names of ships from Nelson's fleet: Victory, Reliance and Soverin (sic).

But back to Robin Hood once more, for there are more and intriguing connections with the outlaw further up the Derwent valley. At Hathersage you can toast another of the Merrie Men at the Little John Hotel. The corner pub was originally called the Butcher's Arms, and also the Drum and Monkey, then with the arrival of the railway it changed its name to the Station Hotel.

Landlord George Dakin standing outside the Station Hotel in Hathersage during the mid 1920s. Originally called the Butcher's Arms, it presumably changed its name to attract new custom. Today it's called the Little John Hotel.

But in the late 1940s it was renamed in honour of Robin Hood's oversized companion, for according to local legend Little John is supposedly buried in the village churchyard, where there is indeed a grave fully 10 feet long. When the grave was opened in the 1700s it is said that a human thighbone 32 inches long was unearthed. Near Hathersage you will also find Robin Hood's Stoop; above Bradwell is Robin Hood's Cross; and among the gritstone rocks of Stanage Edge there is also Robin Hood's Cave.

There's another larger-than-life character that, for

some reason, is etched into the national psyche, and who also has a connection with the pubs of our region. However, this one didn't exactly rob from the rich to give to the poor – he just robbed.

We start at the Bull's Head in Tintwistle, at the western end of Longdendale, which still boasts that it once entertained the notorious highwayman Dick Turpin. He supposedly dined here on his way back to his Yorkshire home after attending the Manchester Races, and on one occasion they say he even had his horse re-shod at the village smithy. Mind you, such are the stories that have grown up around this inevitably shadowy figure that they all must be taken with a large pinch of salt.

Stand and deliver! Dick Turpin is supposed to have called at the remote Bull i' th' Thorn on the Buxton-Ashbourne road for refreshment.

Interestingly, Dick Turpin (real name John Palmer) was born at a pub – the Bell in the village of Hempstead in north Essex, where his father John was landlord (although the Crown, at Hampstead in north London, also claims this honour). Fittingly, it was also a visit to a pub 34 years later that year that spelled Turpin's ultimate downfall. After a liquid lunch at the George and Dragon in the village of Welton, by the River Humber west of Kingston upon Hull, he went outside into the road and fired off his pistol at a crowing cockerel. Turpin was subsequently arrested and when his true identity was established, the gallows at Tyburn beckoned, and today his bones rest in a grave in the city of York.

The tales surrounding Dick Turpin – even in the Peak District, where he never lived – are legendary. For instance, it is said that apart from visiting Tintwistle, he also called in at the Bull i' th' Thorn pub at Pomeroy; but of course there is no record of his having ridden the Ashbourne to Buxton road. One local highwayman who certainly did was William Buxton, born at Elton, near Winster, and who for a short while terrorised travellers on this popular route. After robbing a stage coach in 1780 he was pursued to Ashbourne, where he was finally arrested outside the Anchor Inn. He was hanged in Derby shortly afterwards.

Although Turpin may not have used this particular route, it is more likely is that he travelled the Chesterfield to Derby road, since Derby in the eighteenth century was already a prosperous market town and not too far from his Yorkshire base. In fact, this historic coach road has numerous associations with the infamous highwayman. There's a Turpin's Road near Makeney (where the Coach and Horses pub was said to have once kept Turpin's pistols); he is supposed to have family connections at Horsley; and Heage Common was notorious as the hideout of a particularly ruthless gang of highwaymen. For further information on this subject make sure to read Peter Elliott's recent book *Dick Turpin in Derbyshire?*

An inn with a view

Although by no means a mountainous region, the Peak District boasts a number of well-sited country pubs from where you can enjoy tremendous views, often stretching over several counties. Some on the western moors, such as the Mermaid Inn and Cat and Fiddle, are described elsewhere (Chapters 5 and 7 respectively); and the Gate Inn near Sutton Lane Ends is featured in Chapter 6.

The Lathkil Hotel has also been alluded to in the previous chapter, for this charming and well-sited establishment near Bakewell which today thrives on the tourist trade was once frequented by hardworking leadminers. In the mid 1800s, James Bateman was the Agent and Mineral Surveyor for both the Alport and Mandale Mining companies, active in Lathkill Dale, and he made the astute decision that since he was paying the miners for their ore he would open a local alehouse so that they could effectively give their money back to him.

In the early days the pub at Over Haddon was called the Miner's Arms, but when the mining declined at the end of the 1800s the name was changed to the Lathkill View, and later the Lathkill Dale Hotel, as successive publicans tried to tap in to the growing tourist market and entice visitors up the hill from Bakewell.

Certainly few other local pubs can boast such a wonderful situation high on the rim of a deep, lush valley (part of the Derbyshire Dales National Nature Reserve) with views out across the gentle hills of the White Peak. Indeed, there are few better bars in the Peak District in which to loiter and admire the panorama, with huge, south-facing

Visitors to the Lathkil Hotel at Over Haddon relax and enjoy the surroundings.

windows in both the main bar and dining room. Surviving photographs of the pub from early last century show a verandah at the front, and lately the long-term landlord, Robert Grigor-Taylor, has created a terraced beer garden next to the building from where you can enjoy the airy view *al fresco*.

When you consider this, plus the tasty lunchtime buffet, and the choice of four or five well-kept real ales (it's been in CAMRA's Good Beer Guide every year since 1983 – the longest consecutive local entry), then it's no wonder that resuming a walk after an indulgent lunchtime stop can be rather difficult.

Finally, you might have noticed that the current spelling of the hotel's name – 'Lathkil' – appears to be missing a second 'l'. According to Robert Grigor-Taylor this is historically accurate. "If you examine the records you will find different spellings," he explains, "and as far as I am concerned this version is the most consistent over recent years. After all, you need look no further than neighbouring Youlgrave to see that even today there is disagreement over the spelling of actual village names." (For the record, it's 'Youlgrave' to most residents, and 'Youlgreave' to everyone else.)

Other pubs that enjoy wide-ranging views include the Thorn Tree Inn (with the whole of Matlock spread out at your feet), the Millstone

Inn (overlooking the Derwent Valley above Hathersage) and the Old Horns Inn at High Bradfield. The last, located on the far north eastern edge of the region in South Yorkshire, sits in the 'higher' part of the village with good views out across the reservoirs that dot the small valley.

However, keeping your eyes peeled is clearly nothing new to the good folk of Bradfield. Nearby is the Church of St Nicholas, which apart from having the largest parish in England also sports a curious eighteenth-century watch house by the entrance to the churchyard. It was built to keep a lookout for nocturnal body-snatchers. The pub probably takes its name from the annual Bradfield fair, since the patron saint of the fair was St Luke, and his symbol was an ox. Presumably the ceremony therefore involved a pair of horns?

A mile or so westwards along the lane you come to another well-placed pub, this time virtually on its own above Strines Reservoir at the head of the valley. Strines Inn sits at 1,015ft (309m) above sea level, and was originally a manor house dating back to at least the sixteenth century when it was home to the Worrall family.

It's located on Mortimer Road, a former packhorse route that in the mid 1770s became a turnpike between Grindleford and Penistone, but not a very successful one, by all accounts. 'Strines' is believed to be an Old English word meaning the meeting of water; although another explanation is that it derives from the 'strides' of stepping stones once used to cross the stream below the inn, but there is little evidence to support this.

The pub was once called the Tailor's Arms, possibly after some of the regular tradesmen who came this way; and despite often being packed at weekends it has clung on to its authentic, period feel, with a series of dark and rambling rooms stuffed with curios and interesting prints. Like many of the Peak's isolated rural pubs it relies heavily on attracting diners, and traditional dishes such as giant Yorkshire puddings and locally-sourced sausages are always popular.

However, when it comes to drinks you may be surprised to discover that the pub is well-known for something other than beer and wine. Famously, the Strines Inn grinds its own house coffee (a blend of 90 per cent Colombian and 10 per cent Italian Dark Roast), and altogether offers visitors nine different coffees to choose from. No wonder that it has been a previous winner of 'Coffee Pub of the Year'.

While the Strines Inn enjoys a pleasant setting, the Barrel Inn at Bretton is surely the most spectacular in terms of views, and at 1,250ft

The Barrel Inn glimpsed through snowdrifts on the first day of Spring, 1979.
(photo by Jack Bricklebank, courtesy of the Derwent Gallery, Grindleford).

At 1,250 feet above sea level, the Barrel Inn at Bretton is the highest pub in Derbyshire.

(381m) it is also the highest pub in Derbyshire (the Cat and Fiddle inn is just in Cheshire, before you ask).

The 400-year-old building was originally a farmhouse and according to an artist had a heather or thatched roof (see the mounted sketch in the bar). It stands on a pronounced ridge known as Eyam Edge, and overlooks a high and bare limestone plateau criss-crossed by drystone walls and dotted with tiny villages such as Wardlow, Foolow and Great Hucklow.

At the far western end of the ridge huge gliders from the Derbyshire and Lancashire Gliding Club regularly take to the skies from their airstrip, for this is a place that is exposed to the elements and where the wind often blows with tremendous force. They say you can see five counties on a clear day, and the sense of space and airiness is overwhelming.

However, an exposed location such as this also has its downsides. In January 1947 the Peak District experienced one of its most severe snowstorms on record, with temperatures plunging to -18 deg. C in Buxton, and drifts as high as 20 feet.

Perhaps not surprisingly the position of the Barrel Inn meant that the awful weather hit it particularly hard. For a long period the pub was *completely* cut off (it varies from 12 days to three weeks depending on whom you ask), but for certain snow was piled up around the pub in enormous drifts so that it covered every window. When help eventually arrived a tunnel had to be dug from the outside to locate the front door and rescue publican Stanley Drewett and his wife. A man from Eyam who managed to struggle up to the pub said it looked like a "huge igloo". Such was the severity of the weather during that winter that blizzards continued on and off until March, and the Barrel was effectively out of bounds for over five weeks.

Elsewhere in the Peak District conditions were equally bad. Earl Sterndale was cut off for almost seven weeks, and the people of Longnor were so desperate for food that an RAF airplane dropped supplies by parachute, with the pilot guided by a bonfire and a large black cross marked out in the snow with soot. Villages and hamlets ran out of supplies, farm animals perished, and a funeral party from Foolow had to be led by a snowplough.

In the Staffordshire village of Grindon, a memorial in the church remembers the crew of another RAF plane which, unfortunately, crashed on Grindon Moor while trying to drop provisions to the isolated community in 1947.

The road that runs along the top of Bretton's panoramic edge was once known as Bretton racecourse, and apparently it was not unusual for horses to be raced up and down this long, straight stretch, and wagers to be taken (then probably spent in the Barrel Inn afterwards). With the long, flat surface and intense clear air, it is said that some horses were trained here for other race meetings.

The ridgetop route has been used for centuries, and was a well-known trading route from Cheshire to Sheffield. Later on the precise route was defined in a popular turnpike, authorised by the Road Act of 1757, which ran from the Barrel eastwards to Sheffield via Ringinglow and Longshaw, and the other way via Great Hucklow, Tideswell and Wormhill to Buxton.

The natural world

Ever since King Charles II escaped his captors by hiding in an oak tree (see Chapter 7), pubs have been named after this most English of trees. But in fact naming the pub or inn after something identifiable that grew outside was nothing new, and long before Charles climbed the Boscobel Oak, clumps of evergreen were being stuck above beerhouse doors to denote their purpose.

Apart from the ubiquitous Royal Oak, there's a Shady Oak at Fernilee, south of Whaley Bridge; a Thorn Tree and Sycamore Inn at Matlock, and two more Sycamores at Birch Vale and Parwich; and finally Yew Tree Inns at Holloway and South Wingfield. The yew was especially significant, since its wood was used to make bows for archers. An Act of Parliament was passed during the reign of Henry V to protect the tree, and it was subsequently planted in churchyards to act as an evergreen symbol of immortality.

As always, it's tempting to assume that the many Yew Tree inns date from this time, but in reality many were probably named much more recently. If any of our pubs should be called the after this tree it should be the Church Inn at Darley Dale. Just across from the pub, on the other side of the railway line, is the twelfth-century St Helen's Church, outside which is believed to be one of the oldest yew trees in Britain. Its 33ft girth is astounding, and estimates of its age vary from 600 to 2,000 years.

Particular places and geographical features like rivers are inevitably commemorated by pubs and inns, including the Goyt Inn at Whaley Bridge and the Manifold Inn at Hulme End. The latter is a handsome, 200-year-old coaching inn by the road bridge over the River Manifold. It stands opposite the old toll house and in previous years has gone through something of an identity crisis, being at one time or other called the Jolly Carter, Wagon and Horses, and the Manifold Valley Hotel. I have even read that it was once named the Light Railway Inn, since the nearby hamlet was the northern terminus of a curious little narrow gauge line called the Leek and Manifold Light Railway which ran between 1904-34.

The Crag Inn at Wildboarclough in Cheshire (see Chapter 2) puts me in mind of rocky slopes and awkward summits, as does Ye Olde Rock Inn at Upper Hulme (and there's another at New Mills), which sits not far from the foot of the mighty outcrop of Hen Cloud at the southern end of the Roaches in Staffordshire. You can stay up for the Star at Tideswell, or the Star Inn Ale House at Glossop, dance over the Moon at Stoney Middleton; and if you've got any energy left (or if the pub goes in for 24-hour opening) witness the Rising Sun at Middleton-by-Wirksworth or Bamford.

Another pub named after a specific local feature is the Lantern Pike Inn at Little Hayfield. It takes its name from the shapely, National Trust-owned hill nearby, since a 'pike' is local dialect for peak or pointed hill, and for some years Lantern Pike was crowned by a beacon which was lit to signal momentous events. The pub is a converted eighteenth-century farmhouse (originally called the New Inn) on the former Buxton-Old Glossop turnpike, and today it's a friendly and unpretentious place that welcomes all comers. It's also stuffed full of curiosities, including a signed letter from *Coronation Street's* original scriptwriter and former local Tony Warren, who supposedly based some of the show's early characters on the pub's regulars.

At nearby Hayfield, the Kinder Lodge, which began life as a weaver's cottage, used to be called the Railway, but changed its name when the line was scrapped. The sign depicts a couple of young ramblers, complete with walking boots and stick, standing by a gap in a drystone wall looking out a large green hill. By rights that hill should be Kinder Scout, I suppose, but where the pub is situated it is more likely to be the aforementioned Lantern Pike.

Not too far away is New Mills, where the Torrs, a grand old pub (sadly given the modern treatment) in the town centre is named after the dramatic Torrs gorge. Here, below the shops and houses, the award-winning Millennium Walkway provides an exciting aerial route above the River Goyt, while the Heritage Centre at the back of the bus station provides more details about the industrial and social heritage of the town.

5
Ghostly Tales and Unusual Goings On

Spirits in the bar?

It should come as no surprise that some of the Peak District's older pubs are reputed to be haunted, but differentiating fact from fiction – especially after the witnesses have had a drink or two – isn't always easy. It's not hard to imagine ghostly goings-on in the long-established public houses, with their chequered histories and array of guests, not to mention the dark corners and creaking passageways. As we shall see, a resident ghost can be very good for business, something not always appreciated at the time by those who experience first-hand a ghoulish apparition or strange phenomenon.

There are some pubs that really do lend themselves to ghost stories, but at Ye Olde Gate Inne at Brassington the tales are more real than most. Situated in this quiet, attractive former lead mining village near Wirksworth, the pub was built in 1616 and substantially altered in 1874. There used to be a tollhouse on the opposite side of the road, so it is likely that the pub took its name from the gate across the road. Apparently there was a small window specially constructed in the side of the pub where passing coachmen would be served a drink.

Almost four centuries on, and a cursory glance inside would lead you to suspect that little has changed. There's a traditional range at the far end of the main room, with scrubbed wooden tables along each side and a stone-flagged floor. Together with the low ceiling and exposed beams, the subdued lighting (and, it must be said, an absence of piped music and fruit machines) means that the pub exudes atmosphere, and nowhere more so than downstairs in the old dining room with its wall-to-wall oak panels and open fireplace.

The landlord, Paul Burlinson, began by telling me about the experiences of some of his guests. "Not so long ago there were two lads who took their drinks into the old dining room," said Paul. "Suddenly they rushed out ashen-faced, saying that they'd seen a mysterious old woman sitting by the fireside in turn-of-the-century dress. They were that scared they left the pub immediately and didn't even finish their drinks – and it was only their first!"

The little-changed interior of Ye Olde Gate Inne at Brassington, reputedly one of the most haunted pubs in the Peak District.

The simple doorway of Ye Olde Gate Inne hides some purportedly spooky customers.

The building has witnessed centuries of comings and goings, reaching as far back as the Civil War when it was used as a temporary hospital after a nearby skirmish. You can't help feeling that if ever there was a pub custom-made for ghosts then surely it's the Olde Gate Inne.

Perhaps not surprisingly, therefore, a number of customers have reported mysterious sightings and odd feelings while visiting the pub, so much so that a previous landlady invited an exorcist to rid the building of ghosts (apparently unsuccessfully), and in 1998 a team of paranormal experts spent a night in the pub to record the goings-on using digital cameras and EMF (electro-magnetic field) equipment. They concluded that there was without doubt unusual and unexplained activity, and they noted the heavy atmosphere and sudden drops in temperature, rushes of cold air and the way their candles would oddly flare and flicker. One complained of piercing headaches, another that he felt he was being hit on the head with a heavy weapon, while a third was convinced that she kept on hearing the nearby sound of stabled horses. It's not recorded how much they had to drink.

Haunted houses

Many pubs claim to have ghosts, although some of these non-alcoholic spirits are a little more friendly than others. One of the upstairs bedrooms at the Wheatsheaf Hotel at Baslow is haunted by an ostler (a man employed to look after the horses at a coaching inn) who occasionally makes the journey across from the courtyard stables to the main building – except that the bridge that he uses that once connected the former stables disappeared many years ago. Apparently he has been seen more than once passing through the outside wall and moving across the bedroom.

Meanwhile, the Eyre Arms at Hassop is home to the ghost of a Cavalier who supposedly hid in an upstairs priest's hole to avoid being captured, since the Eyre family's seat at Hassop Hall was a Royalist stronghold during the Civil War. This malevolent, ill-tempered apparition still descends the stairs (now long-gone), runs down behind the bar, then goes out into the road.

There he is sometimes joined by a coach and horses, and according to a local tale, a passing motorist was once killed trying to swerve to avoid them. Before he expired he managed to explain that the horse-drawn carriage appeared to be coming straight towards him, and then afterwards vanished into thin air. On another occasion, one dark evening in the 1980s, a distraught stranger rushed into the pub saying that he had just run someone over with his car. Of course, everyone immediately went outside to help, but as hard as they looked, no-one was ever found.

Incidentally, the Eyre family is also associated with Highlow Hall, south west of Hathersage, once described by local author Roy Christian as "reputedly the most haunted house in Derbyshire". It's supposedly troubled by all manner of ghostly forms, including a murdered servant and the White Lady who came to a brutal and untimely end long ago in a bedroom.

The Old Nag's Head at Edale has been spooked by more recent events, if you believe certain people. Over the last 75 years a large number of aircraft have crashed on the high and treacherous moors of Kinder Scout and Bleaklow, and especially during the Second World War. Many were Allied planes returning from bombing missions, and due to bad weather and unfamiliar terrain they came to grief on the 2,000ft-high hills. After one such crash, the bodies of the RAF bomber crew were retrieved and carried down to the Old Nag's Head. Since then, several customers have reported seeing ghostly figures in airmen's uniform, and there have been unidentifiable sounds and voices around the pub.

A ghoulish woman dressed all in black is supposed to haunt the Travellers Rest pub in the Hope Valley, located opposite the turning to Bradwell. They say she died after falling down a spiral staircase while trying to escape the clutches of a drunken labourer on Christmas eve many years ago, and can be witnessed each year on that same night, gliding along the upstairs corridor holding a bunch of keys.

The Duke of York, a pub on the Ashbourne-Buxton road at Pomeroy, is haunted by the ghost of William Pomeroy, a local man who was killed in a horse-riding accident on the roadway outside several centuries ago. Apparently he is responsible for switching the kettle on when there's no-one around, hiding car keys, and everyday things like that. Meanwhile a short distance away near Hurdlow is the Bull i'th'Thorn, which is said to host a young ghost called Jenny who sits on the slipper box.

Ghostly girls also feature at the Miner's Arms at Eyam, which despite the village's reputation surrounding the visitation of the Plague, seems to be doing well enough with unrelated ghouls and phantoms. The two little sisters are called Sarah and Emily, and they died when fire consumed the run-down shack which stood on the site of what later became the pub. One of the girls died in the fire, started accidentally when they were playing with a candle, and the other fell down a hidden mineshaft while trying to escape.

Landlady Michele Hunt says that guests staying in Room 6 have reported hearing a girl shouting out the name "Emily!", while others speak about strange noises, especially footsteps, and unexplained cold spots. "People come here specifically to stay in the haunted room," she says, "while others learn of the stories once they get here and are too scared to go back to their room. You have to be a believer, of course, but we've never heard or seen anything ourselves, because we live in the cottage next door and not on the premises."

A previous landlord said he heard a clock being wound up in the early hours, and his daughter's record player began playing in an empty room. He also reported that the air on the landing was always cold, despite his repeated efforts to heat it, and that his family all heard the mysterious sound of heavy footsteps and rustling of a skirt in the corridor outside – even though it was thickly-covered by deep-pile carpet. Only later did it come to light that over 200 years ago an earlier landlord murdered his wife by forcing her along the landing and pushing her downstairs.

This may also be the apparition encountered by a former chairman of the parish council, who reported seeing an elderly woman dressed in a bonnet and old-fashioned clothes enter the building not long after it had been refurbished. Apparently she wandered about in a confused state for some time before vanishing into thin air.

A ghost dressed in Victorian clothes and known as Old Sarah is purported to roam the George Hotel in Tideswell late at night in search of her long-lost husband, and once scared away an entire party of guests in the 1930s. The Highwayman, a delightful sixteenth-century inn on the Macclesfield-Whaley Bridge road near Rainow, has a ghostly old man who is sometimes to be seen sitting on his own in the corner of the snug; while in the middle room, mysterious smoke rings often appear even though no-one is present.

A young girl supposedly haunts the Rising Sun at Middleton-by-Wirksworth, and it is said that in the 1950s when the landlord was undertaking some rebuilding work he came across a secret bedroom boarded up and hidden away. Meanwhile, the Strines Inn in South Yorkshire is said to be haunted by a Grey Lady who can be seen wandering along the former driveway in a melancholy fashion.

The Derwentwater Arms at Calver is another pub which is supposed to be haunted, but the ghost in question is actually a previous landlord.

Apparently he was fond of practical jokes, and one day pretended to be dead by lying motionless under a sheet in the bar (not exactly the best way to encourage custom, it must be said). However, his just desserts came the next day. He was travelling back from Bakewell market when he fell from his horse and was killed, and his ghostly presence is supposed to remain in the building.

A long-departed landlord is supposed to still frequent the Queen Anne at Great Hucklow, where he apparently died in the cellar; while in Bakewell the Peacock Hotel is prone to mischievous pranks of a former landlord's daughter from the 1840s. The girl, called Harriet, is often blamed for turning off the beer pumps and switching lights on or off.

According to Nicky Crewe, who leads regular 'ghost walks' in the town, another of Bakewell's haunted pubs is the Wheatsheaf, on Bridge Street. She says that here the supernatural presence is through smell, with customers reporting the sharp and unpleasant smell of rough pipe tobacco in otherwise empty rooms. Apparently it's the same brand used by a pipe-smoking former regular, long since departed for the great public house in the sky.

"Old pubs and inns are a common place to find ghosts and unexplained happenings," says Nicky, who recently completed an M.A. in folklore and cultural traditions at Sheffield University. "They are a great example of what are known as 'liminal' places, which means that they represent a threshold or a crossing-point of different forces. With their cellars, attics, stairs and corridors, not to mention all the people who pass through them over the years, they provide an interface between two worlds."

Other pubs that are reputedly haunted include the Stanhope Arms at Dunford Bridge, which is troubled by a ghost called Mary whose husband was killed in the building of the Woodhead Tunnel; and at the Square and Compass at Darley Bridge, a previous landlord assured me that the pub was in the grip of a mischievous spirit who made doors open and close on their own. I suggested it might just be the wind.

People have also spoken of ghostly goings-on at the Miner's Standard, in Winster. They take the form of unexplained noises, such as footsteps in empty rooms and doors creaking. Others report hearing a girl (apparently called Mary) singing 'Three Blind Mice', although I have found another source which claims it is sung in the weak and shaky voice of an old woman. Either way, there is a framed parchment on the wall with more background to these mysterious happenings.

Mind you, pub-goers in Winster might be relieved that they no longer have to set foot in the Angel Inn, which once occupied the three-storeyed building opposite the old Market House. According to local tales, the pub was haunted by a headless bride in a wedding dress. One woman spied her in a mirror while putting on make-up, and such was the shock that she fainted with fright (well, you would, wouldn't you?).

Spooky nuptials also concern nearby Winster Hall, for a while a pub in the 1980s and early '90s. Apparently it is haunted by two young lovers, the well-to-do daughter of the house and the lowly coachman, whose relationship was frowned upon and the union strictly forbidden. Instead, marriage to another man was hastily arranged, but the night before the wedding the two sweethearts flung themselves off the balustrade to their death. Inevitably their ghosts remain, and the Hall is sometimes referred to as Lover's Leap. Other stories tell of long-locked doors suddenly found opened, and strange noises in the night. A soldier who was billeted at the Hall during the Second World War was so alarmed by a nocturnal apparition that he fired off his revolver at it.

If you stay at the Red Lion at Wirksworth be prepared to bump into a headless coachman dressed in a dark green cloak and striding along the corridor or wandering about the yard. This unfortunate man met his end a couple of centuries back, when the pub was a busy coaching inn. The story goes that he was approaching the pub, as usual sitting high up on his box, when for some reason the horses bolted forwards under the archway and the coachman didn't duck in time... ouch!

In terms of the sheer number of sightings, however, probably the most haunted pub in the Peak District is the Castle Hotel at Castleton, which is rumoured to have as many as four separate ghosts. A bustling and popular place in the daytime and early evening, this former seven-teenth-century coaching inn has some more unusual guests at other times – if you believe the stories.

There's the small, elderly woman called Agnes, about five foot four and who wears her hair in a bun. She is supposed to be have been a former housekeeper, and walks around the pub in a black uniform and white apron. Another story relates to a soldier and a nurse who have been seen in the cellar; while two former licensees reports witnessing a man in a blue pin-striped suit near the (now closed) side entrance.

He was a local man called Mr Cooper, who lived on nearby Castle Street and regularly popped into the pub for a drink in the early 1900s. However, because his wife didn't approve, he tried to be discreet and always used the side entrance. The story goes on to relate how, by trade, he was a miner, but on Sunday he would dress up in his best outfit to enjoy a leisurely drink at the pub. He died, of course, on a Sunday, wearing the pin striped suit.

In both instances, witnesses describe how the apparitions of Agnes and Mr Cooper simply vanished into thin air. There is also a newspaper report from 1962 recounting how the Castle's new landlord and a friend both saw a hazy figure of a woman appearing to wade waist-deep and without any difficulty through the floorboards of the corridor. A later inspection of the building revealed that the corridor had been raised during earlier structural work, and that the ghostly figure was probably walking along the level of the original floor.

However, if you want the full-on experience – and have already survived Room 6 of the Miner's Arms at Eyam – then book yourself into Room 4 of the Castle Hotel. It's located upstairs on the front corner of the building, overlooking the road, and is reportedly haunted by a Grey Lady called Rose.

One explanation is that she was a chambermaid at the hotel who tended its gardens and sold flowers to the guests; but the more common version is of her as a jilted bride. She supposedly walks along the corridor to the dining room to have her wedding breakfast, which of course was abandoned when the ceremony was called off. One servant who saw her gliding along the corridor in a white gown and a veil fled the building screaming, while staff say that many guests have reported feeling something creepy and unsettling in and around the room. What is remarkable is that these encounters have continued right up to the present day, so much so that there was a séance held in Room 4 in May 1999, when spiritualists believed they made contact with the unfortunate Rose.

Mermaids and murders

There are other pubs that while not haunted themselves, are associated with strange or dastardly tales. The Mermaid Inn sits high and isolated on a bleak Staffordshire ridge in the south west corner of the Peak District above the village of Thorncliffe. On a clear day the views are superb, and they say you can even see the mountains of North Wales; but when the biting wind rattles in or the mist is swirling off the desolate moorland it feels unwelcoming and even sinister.

The pub was originally known as Blakemere House, after a nearby moorland pool called Blake Mere, and it is here in the dark and supposedly bottomless waters that the tragic and grisly tales emanate. According to legend, a man called Joshua Linnet drowned a beautiful young woman in the pool, believing her to be a witch. As she disappeared beneath the waters it is said that she had a look of the Devil, screaming vengeance on Linnet. Three days later he was found dead, drowned in Blake Mere, his face seared as if by talons. Ever since then the siren has haunted the pool, appearing at midnight to haul the unsuspecting into the depths. The saying goes:

She calls on you to greet her
combing her dripping crown
and if you go to greet her,
She ups and drags you down.

Another, often-repeated story, tells how a local farmer, a little the worse for wear after a few drinks in the Cock Inn at Leek, boasted that he would fearlessly walk across the moors to the pool. A wager was struck, and the farmer set off through the mist. Nearing the pool he heard the cries of a woman, and came across a man kneeling by the poolside attempting to strangle her.

Seeing the farmer, the man ran off, after which the farmer carried the terrified woman to the nearby Mermaid Inn. She explained that her assailant was the father of her unborn child, who ashamed of her pregnancy wanted to do away with them both. Luckily the woman was saved and the farmer claimed his five shillings winnings.

They say that no bird or animal will drink from the pool, and that it's never been known to freeze over in winter nor dry out in the hottest summer. Either way, the mermaid of Blake Mere must be unique, living a sizeable distance from any ocean as well as 1,600ft above sea level.

Another local legend tells of headless horseman who gallops across the moors and grabs poor, unfortunate souls and drags them off to their doom. Is he one of the Four Horsemen of the Apocalypse? Or is he, as others would have it, the decapitated remains of a local soldier whose faithful horse brought him back from battle? Or perhaps he just has a habit of appearing to those already well acquainted with another kind of spirit at the Mermaid Inn?

Incidentally, if you're still a convinced sceptic and you think that all this is a load of 'cock and bull', you might be interested to know that this everyday expression comes from a pub setting. The Cock and the Bull were rival pubs at Stony Stratford in Buckinghamshire, but such was the competition that news and gossip picked up at one was quickly exchanged with customers from the other. Of course, things got exaggerated in the telling, so that the more preposterous sounding tales became known as a 'cock and bull story'.

Other pubs have also been associated with grisly goings on. A Scottish pedlar (they were often called 'Scottish' because they sold cheap Scottish linen) met an untimely end at the Moon Inn at Stoney Middleton, when two rival pedlars – jealous of his success at the Eyam Wakes – dragged him outside and, it is believed, did away with him. Two decades later his body was eventually discovered in a nearby cave and identified by his distinctive buckled shoes. The man's bones were removed to Eyam Church where they were later buried, while his shoes were taken away and worn by a local bellringer.

In 1679, Andrew Simpson served as an ostler at the Red Lion at Leek, but he had an ulterior motive for getting to know the inn's wealthier customers, for he was also a robber on the side. One of his luckless victims was a woman pedlar from Bakewell who had come to Leek market to sell thread and cloth. Aware that she had made some money before returning home, Simpson ambushed her on the moors above Leek at Blake Mere, then strangled the poor woman before weighing her body down and throwing her in the pool. But he made the mistake of giving away some of the stolen linen and lace to a maidservant at the Mermaid Inn, and after this was traced and the pool dragged for her body, Simpson was arrested and hanged for murder.

Another gruesome event was the so-called Winnats Murder, when a young couple running away to get married at the church at Peak Forest (see Chapter 4) met their untimely end in the spectacular limestone gorge of the Winnats Pass near Castleton in 1758.

Allan and Clara were first documented stopping at the Royal Oak Inn at Stoney Middleton to feed their horses, but it was while they dining at an inn at Castleton that they were sized up by a group of drunken miners who had noticed the well-off strangers whom they suspected of carrying money and valuables. They laid in wait for the couple further up the valley by Odin Mine, and dragging them into a barn proceeded to rob and murder them.

The bodies were eventually thrown down the mineshaft and discovered a decade later; but according to the well-known story, although the five miners were never made accountable for their crimes, they all lived out sad and desperate lives after the double murder. One was later killed by a falling stone near the scene of the crime, another broke his neck in an accident, a third committed suicide, the fourth third went insane and the last made a death-bed confession. It is said that on stormy nights you can still hear the ghosts of Allan and Clara wailing in the Winnats Pass, and what is purported to be Clara's red leather saddle is on show in the shop of Speedwell Cavern at the foot of the Pass.

Another location that, in certain conditions, can feel bleak and rather inhospitable, evoking an eerie and even sinister atmosphere, is Wardlow Mires. It's a bare limestone plateau between Tideswell and Eyam and home to the renowned Three Stags Heads, described in Chapter 2; and if ever there was a pub that fitted its landscape then this is it.

The name of the location is hardly redolent of sunny dales and tinkling streams, so no wonder that it was once the haunt of highwaymen who used to prey on travellers using the Chesterfield to Manchester route. Indeed, for some people the gloomy and unwelcoming feel to the place is associated with these shady characters and their crimes – the results of which were often grisly.

Perhaps the most notorious outlaw was Black Harry, a local highwayman who frequented the Bull's Head in the nearby village of Wardlow. He stood and delivered for the last time around 1700, and after being apprehended he was hanged and gibbeted, with the gibbet post erected opposite the Three Stags Heads.

The same fate awaited 21-year-old Anthony Lingard from Tideswell who, in 1815, was in fact the last person to be gibbeted in Derbyshire. He had been convicted of the brutal murder of Hannah Oliver, the tollkeeper of the Wardlow Mires turnpike. Her body was discovered by the landlady of the Three Stags Heads, and it is said that a few days later Lingard actually watched the funeral procession pass by from the doorway of a pub. Unfortunately for him he was arrested after a pair of new red shoes he had taken from Mrs Oliver for his girlfriend were found at his home (a shoemaker from Stoney Middleton identified them as a pair he had made for the late tollkeeper).

He was tried at Derby Assizes, found guilty and hanged. Afterwards, Lingard's corpse was brought back in a cart to a gibbet near Wardlow Mires under military escort. According to eyewitness accounts, there was something of a carnival atmosphere at Wardlow, with stalls and entertainers. A preacher called John Longden, who that day had walked 15 miles to preach at Tideswell only to find the chapel empty, carried on to Wardlow and instead conducted an impromptu outdoor sermon (interestingly, he was later to become the landlord at the Snake Inn). Lingard's bones rattled in their metal cage in what is still known as Gibbet Field, near Peter's Stone, for eleven years.

In 1927, the landlady of the Lantern Pike Inn (then called the New

Inn) at Little Hayfield, 36-year-old Amy Collinson, was brutally murdered on the premises. Her husband had gone out for the day, and when he arrived back he found Amos Dawson, one of the pub's regulars, standing puzzled on the doorstep wondering why the pub wasn't yet open. Inside they found Amy lying in a pool of blood, a knife stuck in her throat.

The police soon found that a small amount of money was missing – less than £40 – and as they began to interview local men, including the pub's regular customers, suspicion began to fall on George Hayward. He was unemployed and in debt, and a witness remembered seeing Hayward on the morning of the murder wearing a black mac, even though it was dry. Hayward explained that he had called into the pub for cigarettes that morning before catching the bus to New Mills to collect his dole. However, another neighbour had seen Hayward cutting a lead pipe outside his home, and the matching length of piping was then located in the water cistern at the pub. There were also blood stains on Hayward's hat that matched the landlady's blood group, and a search of his house revealed money stuffed up the chimney. It seemed pretty conclusive.

In February 1928 Hayward was tried at Derby Assizes, and even though the trial had to be restarted after a juryman collapsed when listening to the gory details of the murder, Hayward was found guilty and was hanged by Thomas Pierrepoint in March 1928.

Odd and odder

Sometimes the goings-on at particular hostelries in the Peak District are not so much spooky or morbid as just plain odd, and there are several peculiar annual 'competitions' which are held at or from pubs that certainly do not feature at any Olympics.

Now, you may have heard of the World Conker championships (held at the Chequered Skipper pub in Ashton, near Oundle in Cambridgeshire, by the way), but every year at a pub in the south of the Peak District they hold the official World Toe-Wrestling Championships.

The event began at the Olde Royal Oak at Wetton, a pleasant village south west of Hartington which is very popular with walkers exploring the Manifold valley and its dramatic natural features such as Thor's Cave. There's even shelving by the front door of the pub expressly for rucksacks and dirty boots.

However, in past years, walkers who dropped by on a particular summer's weekend would be surprised to find that they weren't the only ones massaging their hot and aching feet. In fact, they could well be treated to the sight of a large and animated group of people taking off their shoes and socks to see who had the most powerful toes in the world.

It is said that toe wrestling began in 1976 when regulars at the Olde Royal Oak decided to search for a game that the British could win. It loosely resembles arm wrestling (except with toes, of course), with competitors locking digits in an attempt to force over an opponent's foot on a 'toe-dium' in the best of three 'toe-downs.' Apparently, if a competitor is in too much pain he or she can give in by shouting out the words "Toe Much!"

There are men's and ladies categories, and such is the publicity that the contest attracts entrants, not to mention the media, from around the world. According to local legend, the championships were abandoned in 1977 after a Canadian tourist rather unsportingly won the title; but they were resurrected in the 1990s when a new landlord at the Royal Oake discovered the original rules.

Entrants have toe-curling nicknames (if you excuse the pun) like Paul 'The Toeminator' Beech, the 2004 men's winner. At the same event, sponsored by an international ice cream chain, the founders of the original event, George Burgess and Brian Holmes, were awarded Lifetime Achievement Awards from "all who have been touched by toes". (If all this is getting a bit much, then at least draw heart from the fact that the day's contest is also an excuse for some vigorous charity fundraising for worthy local causes.)

In 2004 the championships moved to the Bentley Brook Inn at Fenny Bentley, a few miles away, and with a new landlord at the Olde Royal Oak it's unclear whether they will return to their spiritual home or stay at the Bentley Brook.

The Peak District is generally not known for its race meetings, with just a handful of annual events like the point-to-point Flagg Races, and harness racing at Pikehall. (Regulars at the Horse and Jockey public house at Tideswell have quite a long trek to their nearest race course!) However, at the village of Bonsall, near Matlock, a more unusual type of racing takes place on the first Saturday of August every year, when chickens are raced across the car park outside the Barley Mow. Yes – I did say chickens.

The pub is situated on The Dale, off Bonsall's long and winding main street, and is comprehensively but tastefully furnished – albeit with hen memorabilia – and offers a cosy fireside in winter and some lovely seats out on the terrace in summer. There's also regular live music and a well-kept pint of beer; and it's one of the few Peak District pubs that has been specifically mentioned in a best-selling work of modern fiction (*Pastures Nouveaux* by Wendy Holden).

However, the summer-time spectacle of live hens racing each other outside is probably the most compelling activity associated with the pub. It's free to watch and anyone with a hen can enter, and in past years as many as 30 birds have been lined up at the start. The hens are cajoled down a narrow track between plastic safety fences, with their owners shouting and hollering encouragement and offering handfuls of feed at the far end beyond the winning line.

However, hen racing is not the only strange thing happening in these parts. The Barley Mow's larger-than-life landlord, Alan Webster, leads Bank Holiday walks in and around the village, and is a fund of fascinating information about the area. In particular, he will regale you with tales of the strange lights spotted above nearby Slaley Moor, reported so often and with such conviction that Bonsall has made national news and UFO-spotters come to the location from all over the country to gaze up at the heavens.

Over 100 unidentified sightings have been recorded in the skies above Bonsall and Slaley in the past 30 years. The International Bonsall UFO Society meet at the pub, and Alan keeps a careful note of any sightings reported to him. He's even been interviewed on the BBC over the suspected UFO sightings. However, the only alien you are most likely to encounter in Bonsall is the shiny inflatable little chap who sits behind the bar.

There's a peculiar challenge that takes place inside the Peels Arms at Padfield, near Glossop. According to the present landlady, it began around the 1950s when workmen, who were staying in the area to erect new electricity pylons and had been 'relaxing' in the pub at the end of the day, dared each other to squeeze through a small hole in the wall of the bar. The gap in question is through an interior wall next to the main bar, and measures about two feet deep by about one across, and is vaguely keyhole-shaped. It was presumably left as a decorative feature and formerly held a vase.

After the workmen successfully squeezed through the tiny opening a new past-time was born: known as 'holing'. Although it seems so small only a child would fit through (and many do), apparently plenty of adults manage the feat, although one or two sometimes get stuck and need a helping hand. There's a special knack to holing. You have to go head-first, from one direction only (aiming towards the bar), and with one arm out front you twist your body through the fissure.

Successful holers used to get a free pint of beer, but this was stopped after the pub's barrels began to empty rather too fast, and now you receive a special certificate to commemorate your achievement. It's headed 'The Order of the Hole', and records that so and so '...has passed through the Hole under the watchful eyes of the Hole-Minders'. The Hole-Minders are, inevitably, the locals, who offer advice and encouragement, and no doubt look on with some amusement. I guess it beats watching the football on the pub TV.

A highly unusual, and many would say unnecessarily gruelling, outdoors event involving pubs and beer has been occurring in the Dark Peak every October for the last few years. It all began one day after the regulars of the Old Nag's Head at Edale realised that the unimaginable had happened: the pub had run dry.

Rather than stare disconsolately into their empty pint glasses, they decided to go in search of a fresh barrel of beer and headed off on foot for the Snake Pass Inn. Although only four and half miles away, there's the small matter of Kinder Scout in between, and this 2,000ft barrier (complete with steep slopes and the hags and groughs of Kinder's infamous blanket bog) proved rather testing, especially when propelling a full beer barrel. Still, the thirsty team completed the exercise, and apparently so enjoyed the occasion that the Great Kinder Beer Barrel Challenge was born.

Today, teams of eight race between the Snake Inn and the Nag's Head carrying a nine-gallon beer barrel (called a firkin and weighing 98lb/44kg) on a home-made stretcher or similar contraption. The event raises plenty of money for local charities, with the aching winners coming away with a trophy and, most appropriately, a free firkin of beer for their efforts.

The Riverhead Brewery Tap at Marsden in West Yorkshire (see chapter 8) organises an annual celebration of Cuckoo Day each April. It remembers the old cuckoo legend, which tells how the good people of Marsden thought that if they captured a cuckoo they would also be able to usher in the spring, since the one is said to herald the other. So when a group of local men saw a cuckoo in a tree they decided to build a wall around it in order to capture the bird, but just as they put the last stone in place it flew up and away. The men were understandably upset, but their leader turned round to the others and said that they must have built the wall too low.

Cuckoo Day begins with a walk to the purported birthplace of the Marsden cuckoo, then in the evening there is a folk concert at the pub, when a specially-brewed beer called 'Ruffled Feathers' is sold. Various activities and events are held on the Saturday, including craft fairs, clog dancing and a duck race, and it all culminates in the Grand Cuckoo Procession – with plenty of special cuckoo hats on show.

Interestingly, the cuckoo story is not unique to Marsden. In medieval times a group of purported lunatics lived in woods near the village of Gotham, in Nottinghamshire, and on one occasion tried to hedge in a cuckoo so it would sing to them all year round. Of course, the bird flew off, and like their Marsden counterparts they blamed themselves for not making the hedge high enough. This and other strange antics (such as trying to drown fish in buckets of water and burning down a forge to rid it of a wasps' nest) were recorded in a book that for a while made the area quite well-known, so that the notion of a 'cuckoo pen' became a joke name given to a small hillside croft or enclosure. Fittingly, the village pub at Gotham is called the Cuckoo Bush.

The Derby Tup

There's a live performance that is believed to be unique to Derbyshire and its pubs, but sadly it is rarely seen these days. Until the 1960s it was still fairly common to encounter a group of four young men touring Derbyshire pubs around Christmas to earn some extra money by putting on the 'Derby Tup' (also known as the 'Old Tup' or 'Derby Ram'). The performance involved miming and singing and began with a plea from the four men for beer:

> Here comes me and my old lass,
> Short o'money, short o'brass;
> Pay for a pint and let's all sup,
> Then we'll show you our jolly Old Tup.

The last two lines sometimes appeared as:

> Gather around us and come close up,
> And we will perform you the Derby Tup.

The origins of the performance are unknown, but the ballad was familiar as far back as the eighteenth century, and was particularly common in the north east of the county. Some have conjectured that its roots lie in a guising or mumming play.

The tale surrounds a mother and father taking a tup (a male sheep) to the butchers for slaughter. One of the four men would dress up as the ram, occasionally with just a sackcloth over his head, but at other times with a more elaborate costume involving a real sheep's skull. The second player acted out the part of the butcher, wielding a large stick or knife with which he would pretend to thump the unfortunate beast. The third dressed as a woman and the fourth player had a blackened face and carried a basin. The number of verses varied, but began in similar fashion:

> As I was going to market upon a market day,
> I met the finest ram, Sir, that was ever fed on hay...

The performance took between 10-15 minutes to complete, and involved the tup entering the slaughterhouse and threatening everyone within, while the others made claim and counter-claim about the animal's prowess:

> This tup was fat behind,
> This tup was fat before,
> This tup was ten yards high,
> If not a little more.
>
> The wool that grew upon its back
> It grew so mighty high,
> That eagles built their nest in it
> You could hear the young ones cry.

The words and even the verses tended to vary between locations, and no doubt there was some variation and elaboration depending on how much beer had been consumed; but the end result was usually that the unfortunate tup met his end, with everyone gathering around to discuss what was left:

> All the boys in Derby,
> Came begging for his eyes,
> To punch them out for footballs,
> For they were just a size.

90

And all the women in Derby,
Came begging for his ears,
To make their leather aprons of,
To last them forty years.

In Derby, people use to gild the horns of their rams when performing the play, which has prompted suggestions that it might have some distant connection with the Roman custom of gilding the horns of animals for sacrifice. The performance is rarely acted out these days, which is perhaps a reflection both on the proliferation of pub jukeboxes as well as a waning interest in local traditions and customs. However, since the Derby Tup (or ram) is the mascot and badge of Derby County Football Club, it's likely to remain lodged somewhere in the county's conscience for a while to come.

There's also a fine old pub of the same name at Whittington Moor on the edge of Chesterfield, a favourite of the Chesterfield and District CAMRA group, whose knowledgeable officer, Jim McIntosh, has been responsible for researching most of this fascinating information.

Another traditional performance that was acted out in certain pubs at Christmas and the New Year was the 'Old Horse'. This ancient folk play took the form of an unaccompanied ballad chanted by several men and enacted by one dressed in a black cloak topped by a symbolic, stylised horse's head. In later years the head was described as a large, fearsome-looking papier mâché construction formed around the skull of a blind pony killed when it fell down a quarry. It was fixed on to a broom handle so that the operator, hidden in the material, could work the head and snap the jaws as the story unfolded. The gallant animal would fall to the ground in the throes of death, then miraculously resurrected would rise once more in celebration.

When the enactment was over a hat was passed round, or the men would be offered drinks. The group would visit pubs, farms and well-to-do houses, and it seems to have been centred on north east Derbyshire, especially around Dronfield and what is today the Sheffield suburb of Dore (but part of Derbyshire until 1934). Indeed, the few details that survive are courtesy of the Dore Village Society.

Although its origins are unclear, the Old Horse appears to have survived well into the twentieth century. As with many of these kinds of performances, there was much merry-making and a fair amount of heavy drinking, but on one occasion it ended in tragedy. A report in the *Derbyshire Times* from January 1869 described how a man was lost on the moors following a rendition:

> A number of persons, including James Greenwood and Thomas Oxley, had left Dronfield the previous Thursday to go to Barlow and neighbouring villages, to act in what is well known in Derbyshire as the 'Old Horse'. On Friday evening Greenwood and his comrades visited the Bulls Head Inn, Calver. Words of an angry character are said to have passed between Greenwood and Oxley, which ultimately ended in a fight, and Greenwood leaving the party, as it is supposed, to go home. He was last seen as late as 12 o'clock at night, and being defective in sight and also worse for liquor at the time he left the Inn, it is supposed that he may have (being a stranger) missed his way, and perished on some part of the moors, or otherwise have got into the river Derwent, which was much swollen by the heavy rain falling at the time.

The paper went on to describe his appearance:

> He is of middle stature, with a scar on his left cheek near to the jaw, and had on two coats, one of fustian and a dark overcoat mended at the elbow of one of the sleeves, dark trousers and a pair of light clogs...

The following issue of the *Derbyshire Times* reported that his body had been found in the River Derwent, only a quarter of a mile from the pub.

Out of place

Elsewhere, it is the pub itself which is rather unusual, and sometimes this is down to the way it's furnished. A particularly fine example is the Little Mill Inn at Rowarth, a hamlet secreted away in the rolling green upland between New Mills and Glossop on the north western edge of the Peak. There has been a mill at this location since the early 1600s, but the present building was built in 1781 as a candlewick mill.

The pub was on the lower floor – where it still is today – together with a shop for the millworkers, since there were several other mills in the area. Production ended in 1930 when a disastrous flood swept through, taking with it several buildings and the original water wheel. The replica wheel, 36ft high and with 32 spokes, can be viewed from the terrace by the side of the building and now fully working once more, it's a great sight.

However, this splendid relic of the industrial age has a rival for customers' attention, for situated in the grounds at the other end of the pub is an original, 70ft-long Pullman railway carriage called the 'Derbyshire Belle'. It once saw service on the former Brighton Belle Railway, and still retains the original wood panelling and brass fittings. Today it offers three luxurious, en-suite double rooms for overnight guests, and must surely present the most unusual bed and breakfast accommodation in the Peak District.

Inside the pub the so-called 'Water Wheel Inspector's Bar' is a dark and roomy place with a low ceiling and huge wooden beams. There's a flagged area around the open fire, and the place is decorated with all manner of paintings, pictures and memorabilia, including an African Grey parrot called Jack who sits in a cage at the end of the bar and occasionally squawks (or sometimes, I'm afraid to say, swears). To the side of the bar is an adjoining room that, continuing the railway theme, is furnished with former railway carriage seats and tables from the British Rail era. Older visitors, especially, may find it evokes distant memories of commuting and long distance railway journeys, and it is certainly a most unusual place to eat and drink. But it does help if you are something of a train buff.

Transport is also a theme taken up by other pubs, although at the Church Inn at Darley Dale, north of Matlock, the items are often on display out in the car park across the road, since they are not the sort of thing you could easily accommodate in your average trophy cabinet alongside the dominoes plate and darts cups. The pub, located by the railway crossing in Churchtown, holds occasional summer-time rallies of vintage motor vehicles.

"The local lads just turn up with their vintage lorries, fire engines, cars and bikes," the landlord told me. "There's a couple of Scammells, an AC, Atkinsons - you name it, if it's old and well-loved it'll be here!" Barely a mile away, at Two Dales, the Plough is also the home for the Panthers, a club devoted to classic motorbikes. As their name suggests, the 40 or so members are all proud owners of Panther models, but I understand that owners of other classic bikes are welcome to bring their machines along to the monthly meetings at the pub.

Peak District pubs host plenty of other weird and wonderful groups

Celebrations at the Church Inn at Darley Dale, c 1929.

and associations. From ghost-hunters (New Mills) to Morris dancers (Winster), there's nothing better than a social get-together over a pint. The Hanging Gate inn at Chapel en le Frith was once the meeting place for the Hanging Gate Flying Club, which despite its name was not an exclusive group of daredevil fighter pilots, but the name for the local racing pigeon fanciers. Meanwhile, the Manifold Inn at Hulme End in Staffordshire is the base for the Sheen Tug of War team, whose men's and women's teams were both winners at the 2004 National Indoor Championships at Huddersfield.

Taking the Pledge

As we've seen at Edale, when the barrel runs dry one solution is to hoof it over the moors to another pub and get a full one. But once there was a popular social movement whose aim was to get rid of the barrels entirely and encourage people to abstain from the demon drink. And to that end one solution was to establish temperance pubs and hotels, even though to today's mind the thought of a teetotal publican is as bizarre as a vegetarian butcher.

The London Temperance Society (later the British and Foreign Temperance Society) was founded in 1831, and people were urged to go teetotal and 'take the pledge'. What began as a largely working class movement soon attracted religious groups such as the Salvation Army and the Quakers, and before long there were numerous temperance societies, including the National Temperance Federation and the Irish Temperance League.

In the early days there was something of a split between those who favoured moderation, or just opposed drinking spirits, and the hardliners who advocated total abstinence. But the Victorians' crusading morality helped usher in several Acts of Parliament which steadily began to curb the excesses of the licensed trade. Meanwhile, across the country, temperance inns and hotels were springing up to offer an alternative to the dens of iniquity that were pubs.

There are plenty of examples throughout the Peak District, whether in towns such as Wirksworth, where old picture postcards show a temperance hotel above the shops in the main street, through to remote rural locations such as the Tollemarche Arms near Crowden in Longdendale, and Naylor's Temperance Hotel at Ecton Lea in the Manifold Valley.

The Red Lion (later Finderne House) in the village of Alstonefield became a temperance hotel '…where a bottle of pop was 2d in a nonreturnable bottle with a marble in it'; while the Travellers Rest Inn at Taddington, west of Bakewell, was renamed the Marlborough Temperance Hotel, and included a shop and café as well as accommodation.

As early as 1836, in Matlock, you could stay at Brown's Temperance Hotel and Family Boarding House on Dale Road. It was advertised as being close to Matlock Bridge Railway Station and was run by Miss H. Marriott. It had the added attraction, sadly for lady guests only, of 'Smedley's System of Hydropathic Treatment', the water treatment which had made the town famous.

The Okeover Arms at Mappleton, a picturesque brick-built village on the River Dove near Ashbourne, is named after the Okeover family on whose land it stood. In 1926 its then owner ordered it to stop serving alcohol and become a temperance hotel, a situation only remedied in 1962 when brewers Ind Coope leased the premises. In Ashbourne itself, the town's Temperance Society was established in the 1840s, opening a coffee shop and gradually managing to cut the number of pubs.

Mind you, some individuals managed to see the error of their ways without any help. On Dyehouse Lane in New Mills, between the Pineapple Inn and the White Hart, is a short and unremarkable-looking terraced row. An inconspicuous plaque, high up on the top corner of the last house, proudly records how, in the 1850s, a man called Thomas Handford put the demon drink behind him:

> A working man, a teetotaller for ten years who was formerly a notorious drinker and notorious poacher, has recently invested his sober earnings in the purchase of the town prison which he converted into a comfortable dwelling house. Frequently an inmate of the prison whilst a drunkard and a poacher, he is now owner of the whole and occupier of the premises.

It is dated 1854, and entitled 'A Drunkard's Reform'. What it doesn't say is that Handford's conversion followed a traumatic incident at the Cock Inn, which used to stand next to the prison, when his friend and drinking pal dropped dead beside him. After that Handford chose sobriety and never touched another drop. Let that be a lesson to us all!

6

All Buildings
Great and Small

The grand designs

Pubs tend to come in all shapes and sizes, from the humble roadside inn through to the bustling urban tavern and elegant hotel. The busy coaching inns, by their very nature, tended to be large and often hectic affairs, with sizeable accommodation for guests and equally extensive stabling for their horses. The personnel needed to run such a place was considerable – from the publican, bar staff and maids, through to cooks, cellarmen and ostlers.

As we've seen in Chapter 3, many of these coaching inns have gone on to become popular modern pubs and hotels, but there are still some that stand out from the crowd because of their position and their history. Two of the most prominent, that in many ways dominate their respective towns, are the Rutland Arms in Bakewell and the Green Man and Black's Head Royal Hotel at Ashbourne.

The Rutland Arms Hotel, overlooking Rutland Square in the centre of Bakewell, still boasts 35 en-suite rooms, including some annex rooms. It was built in 1804/5 on the site of the former White Horse Inn.

The new building was an imposing Georgian construction, with the Tuscan portico carved by Bakewell sculptor White Watson. Railings lined the narrow front garden, matching those in Bath Gardens opposite, but all these were removed during the Second World War. For a few years the new tap room was known as the White Horse Bar; then later it became the Rutland Tavern before being sold off. The former stables, located across the road, were converted into extra accommodation.

It has been written that the hotel's distinguished past guests included Jane Austen, who is supposed to have stayed here in 1811 and used Bakewell as a model for the fictitious town of Lambton in *Pride and Prejudice* (the Rutland Arms being the inn where Elizabeth Bennett and Mr Bingley met). Unfortunately there's no hard evidence that any of this is true.

Far more certain, and for a lot of people I suspect of considerably more importance, is the fact that the Rutland Arms was where the

Overlooking Bakewell's main square, the Rutland Arms Hotel was where the famous Bakewell pudding was inadvertently created.

The gallows sign across the road outside the Green Man and Black's Head Royal Hotel in Ashbourne is one of the last surviving in the country.

Bakewell pudding was inadvertently created. The town's famous culinary export originated here in the 1850s, due to the carelessness of the hotel cook. Intending to prepare a strawberry tart, she poured the mixture of eggs over the strawberry jam instead of mixing it into the pastry, and what should have become a tart ended up a pudding. Luckily the result went down well with the guests, and a new gastronomic delicacy was established.

However, the content and whereabouts of the original recipe is hotly disputed, with at least one bakery/cafe claiming to have it locked away in a safe. Despite this, Bakewell puddings are widely available throughout the town, but do remember that they are not *tarts*, which are a completely different (and some would say inferior) product. However, in my opinion, neither go well with beer.

The Green Man and Black's Head Royal Hotel at Ashbourne is not especially notable for any culinary dish, but it does have several other claims to fame, and architecturally-speaking this eighteenth-century hotel is memorable for having one of the few surviving gallows sign left in England. It stretches right across St John Street, the main thoroughfare through the town centre, and whether or not it was ever used as a gallows the impressive and historic construction is certainly a rare sight these days.

Perhaps not surprisingly most pub gallows signs have fallen victim to the changing shape and power of today's road vehicles, as well as stricter modern town planning laws. Although rare today, the gallows sign was once a fairly common sight and came about as publicans competed with each other to produce ever-more impressive and eye-catching advertisements for their premises. First, the swinging boards became larger and more prominent, then they began to stretch out into the highway.

Unfortunately other shopkeepers and traders did the same, and contemporary accounts suggest that simply negotiating the clutter of signs and notices festooned outside commercial premises could be an awkward and sometimes dangerous business. Early in the 1700s, for instance, a gallows sign outside a pub in London collapsed and dragged down the front of the house to which it was attached, killing two bystanders in the street below. Finally, in 1797, legislation was passed requiring the dismantling of signs considered a public hazard.

The Green Man Hotel at Ashbourne is famous for more than just its sign, however. Over the years the pubs of the Peak District have entertained many illustrious visitors, but two of Ashbourne's most notable were Dr Samuel Johnson and his companion and biographer James Boswell. Indeed, a plaque on the outside of the hotel wall records Boswell's visit in September 1777, not least because he afterwards praised the inn and the "mighty civil gentlewoman, curtseying very low." Dr Johnson is supposed to have had the Green Man in mind when he declared: "The tavern chair [is] the throne of human felicity."

Apparently the full and official name of this historic Ashbourne establishment is the Royal Green Man and Blackamoor's Head Commercial and Family Hotel, which is surely one of the longest pub or hotel names in the country. (It certainly beats the Thirteenth Volunteer Mounted Cheshire Rifleman, a Stalybridge pub that is often quoted as holding this record.) The present, three-storey brick building is mainly Georgian and dates from around 1750.

It is, in effect, the result of two separate inns coming together. In 1825 the then landlord bought up his nearest rival, the Blackamoor's Head, only to promptly close it down and add its sign to his own. The 'royal' was added after the young Princess Victoria, together with her mother the Duchess of Kent, briefly stopped at the pub for refreshment in 1832.

Without doubt it was a busy coaching inn, since Ashbourne was on the route from Derby to Manchester, and at the rear was a large yard with extensive stabling. When the stagecoaches began to decline there was an omnibus service from the inn to Derby for a while. At the back of the inn there was also a cockpit for cock-fighting, for this was a place that attracted a wide custom.

In addition to the high volume of passing trade, the hotel was an important venue for local events and served as a meeting place for numerous groups and societies. Local magistrates held Petty Sessions in its assembly rooms every Saturday morning; and every other week the Ashbourne Poor Law Board of Guardians and a local friendly society known as the Female Sick Club also met there to dispense poor relief.

The Peak District has its fair share of old and imposing establishments which serve intoxicating liquor, as the phrase goes, and many of these have already been mentioned in other chapters. The Old Hall Hotel in Hope stands on the site of a medieval hall that once belonged to the Balguy family; and Thomas Balguy also built nearby Aston Hall in 1578. The Maynard Arms above the River Derwent at Grindleford is an impressive building, as is the Charles Cotton Hotel which graces the main square at Hartington.

However, despite appearances to the contrary, not all of these handsome and often historic hotels started out as public houses. The Old

Clubhouse in Buxton, next to the Opera House, was built in 1822 as a gentlemen's club, and with its high-ceilings, lavish staircase and Opera House memorabilia, it's a popular venue for concert guests. The Whitworth Hotel is part of the larger Whitworth Institute named after the famous Victorian industrialist (see Chapter 4); while the Stanhope Arms Inn at Dunford Bridge began life at a shooting lodge (see Chapter 8).

The Royal Hotel at Hayfield is another impressive edifice, located beside the village cricket pitch overlooking the River Sett. However, the hotel was originally built as a parsonage in 1755, becoming the Shoulder of Mutton later that century. In 1805, it was bought by the Park Hall estate and returned to a parsonage, only to revert to a pub when the landowner quarrelled with the church and turned the vicar out!

There are also a number of imposing hotels along the Derwent valley south of Matlock, most of which date from the rise of Matlock Bath as a spa resort in the mid 1800s. For a time, its five thermal springs were all the rage, with trainloads of unhealthy visitors heading for the new hydros and baths that lined the picturesque gorge. Two of the best known are probably the New Bath Hotel and the Temple Hotel, the latter a popular coaching inn which in its day attracted such notables as Lord Byron who purportedly wrote a poem on one of its window panes.

Matlock Bath's success as a centre for the trendy new vogue of hydrotherapy inspired attempts elsewhere, but to no great success. The New Bath Hotel at Bradwell tried to exploit the local saline springs, with the hotel including a new bath house (hence its name). Sadly there were too few visitors to make it a success; but the pub/hotel survives to this day. On a more positive note, Bradwell did enjoy some success on the watery front as the birthplace of Samuel Fox, inventor of the folding umbrella.

Bridging the faith

The Peak District doesn't boast too many castles, of any age, so it's no surprise to find that there are only a couple of pubs so-named. Bakewell's Castle Inn is in memory of a motte and bailey castle which once stood on the small hill just across the bridge over the River Wye. There's nothing left to see today, except a rather jolly picture of a fortification (which seems to be modelled on Peveril Castle at Castleton) on the pub sign outside. The pub was previously called the Commercial and Castle, and for over 100 years hosted a regular horse market. Its three garages abutting the pavement were once stables.

The Castle Hotel at Castleton has a more obvious claim to its name, since you can actually see what's left of the Norman Peveril Castle on the hillside above the village. The solid stone keep, built in 1176, still survives, but it's a fair pull up the steep path from the village below (and probably best to visit *before* that big pub lunch). The Castle Hotel is a pleasant old coaching inn with an attractive garden at the rear; but in case you're thinking of staying overnight (in Room 4, above all) make sure to glance at Chapter 5 for a report on some of the pub's more unusual residents.

In addition to two castle inns, there are also some Peakland pubs named after churches. The Church Inn at Darley Dale is near St Helen's Church and its famous old yew tree (see Chapter 4); while the Church House Inn at Bollington, Cheshire, is a friendly and well-presented back street pub sandwiched between terraced houses on Church Street.

The third pub of this name is opposite the parish church of St John the Baptist in Chelmorton, a remote village four miles south east of Buxton high on the limestone uplands of the central Peak. So high is it, in fact, that Chelmorton's parish church is officially the highest in Derbyshire at 1,209ft (367m). The spire is topped by a locust weather-vane, depicting St John's survival in the wilderness when he got by on locusts and honey. The inside of the church is no less interesting, including stone coffins and a fifteenth-century stone font. The bells were salvaged from the former church at the village of Derwent, which was dismantled in 1952 in order to build the Derwent Reservoir (more on this momentous event below).

The pub was originally known as the Blacksmith's Arms, since it is recorded that in the 1870s the landlord was also the village smithy. After your obligatory stop at the Church Inn make sure to take a stroll around the village. The views from the grassy heights of Chelmorton Low, topped by prehistoric barrows, are superb; and in particular you can appreciate the perfectly-preserved medieval strip pattern of fields which still surrounds the village and which is of such historical value that the Peak District National Park has given it special protection.

Still on the subject of churches and pubs, there's an entertaining tale concerning the Miner's Arms at Eyam. In 1648 the Rev. Hunt was called to the pub to baptise the landlord's sick child. Unfortunately, the man of the cloth joined the assembled crowd afterwards and drank heavily, so much so that he ended up getting married there and then to Anne, the landlord's daughter. Alas, the reverend was already engaged to a lady from Derby, who when she heard about what had happened proceeded to sue him. As a result, Rev. Hunt was forced to flee the vicarage, and he and his new and possibly rather startled wife were forced to live in the church crypt, where they went on to bring up several children.

Castles and churches are not the only man-made structures which are commemorated by Peak District pubs; bridges also feature quite prominently. The Bridge Inn at Calver is a friendly two-bar pub sited next to the historic crossing of the River Derwent. Originally a ford and then a wooden bridge, the old stone construction which had stood for centuries was joined by a modern concrete affair in 1974, which is certainly functional but utterly graceless.

Calver's Bridge Inn celebrates the crossing of the Derwent.

There are also a couple of pubs named after specific bridges. Wye Bridge House at Buxton is located, as you would expect, near a crossing point over the infant River Wye; although with so much urban development, including a prominent railway viaduct, the actual bridge itself is almost forgotten. The river rises not far away at Poole's Cavern on the town's southern edge.

Perhaps the most famous named bridge in the Peak District, or at least the one that gives its name to a pub, is the Yorkshire Bridge. The pub is to be found on the A6013 north of Bamford, and is named after a nearby packhorse bridge, still marked on Ordnance Survey maps, which at one time was said to be the only crossing point over the River Derwent for travellers between Derbyshire and the Yorkshire West Riding. The bridge was on a popular route across the Peak District via the Hope Valley into Sheffield, and trains of packhorses were no doubt once a common sight plodding up the valley.

The pub dates from the 1820s, and today is popular with walkers, as it sits among some fine hill country with paths up on to Win Hill and Kinder Scout to the west and Bamford Moor and Stanage Edge to the east. It's also well-used by fishermen attracted to Ladybower Reservoir, since the huge dam across the valley is only a short distance away.

The story behind the three reservoirs in the Upper Derwent valley – Derwent, Howden and Ladybower – is fascinating, and has a direct relevance to our story since it involves hostelries. First stop for today's pub-goer, after the Yorkshire Bridge Inn, will be the Ladybower Inn.

This is to be found on the A57 Snake Road to Sheffield, near the turning for Bamford by Ladybower Reservoir itself. Believed to have once been a farmstead, the roadside inn was originally sited a little further up Ladybower Brook, but moved to its present position about a century ago. The interior of the pub includes prints and photographs connected with the valley and the reservoir; but if you think fishing and Lancaster bombers are odd bedfellows you must first understand a little more about the recent history of the Upper Derwent.

The three mighty reservoirs you see today were built to provide drinking water for the growing cities of Sheffield and the East Midlands, and work started on the first two, the Howden and Derwent dams, in 1901. Forty-four years later, the last of the three (Ladybower) was officially opened, with King George VI and Queen Elizabeth unveiling the new, 140ft (43m) dam. However, the creation of these huge reservoirs came at a cost.

The village of Ashopton, including the historic Ashopton Inn, was demolished, and what little remains now sits beneath 6,310 million gallons (27.9 cubic metres) of water contained in the Ladybower Reservoir. That's pretty final, in anyone's books. There's more on the demise of the Ashopton Inn in Chapter 8.

Inevitably, the first two masonry dams were such a huge construction project that a whole community of navvies was established in the valley, as well as a railway to bring in the stone and raw materials for the dams. The purpose-built settlement was called Birchinlee, nick-named 'Tin Town' after the corrugated iron-clad huts in which some of the workers lived, and it survived for 15 short years.

Although long-vanished, the outline of the 1,000-population 'village' can still be seen among the trees above the road on the west bank of Derwent Reservoir. Perhaps most remarkably of all, for all its well-developed facilities which included shops, school, mission and hospital, Birchinlee deliberately had no pub or alehouse, and beer was usually only served with meals in the canteen.

On the surface of the Ladybower Reservoir you will see a series of fish cages, established and managed by Severn Trent Water for the rearing of trout, since fishing is an important recreational pursuit here. However, many older people will also associate the two upper dams and reservoirs of the Upper Derwent with the Second World War, since they were used by the 617 'Dambusters' squadron for training because of the dale's resemblance to the narrow German valleys which were impounded by the Mohne, Sorpe and Eder dams. A small memorial museum is housed in the West Tower of Derwent Dam, and photographs here and in the local pubs show the last flying Lancaster bomber swooping low over the water as part of anniversary fly-pasts in recent years.

The Ladybower Inn, like the Yorkshire Bridge Inn and Bridge Inn at Calver, are all associated with the River Derwent, the Peak's mightiest waterway. It runs for around 50 miles from its source high up on the boggy, open waste of Featherbed Moss on Bleaklow all the way south to its confluence with the River Trent at Shardlow, near Derby.

Now you can trace the river's journey on foot using the Derwent Valley Heritage Way, a newly-opened recreational route from Ladybower Reservoir south via Chatsworth and the Derwent Valley Mills World Heritage Site. It can be walked continuously or enjoyed in shorter bursts, either as circular walks or using the good public transport services throughout the valley. Not surprisingly, the Heritage Way goes past plenty of pubs, so build plenty of time into your schedule for refreshment stops.

In its journey through the Peak District, the River Derwent is celebrated by pubs bearing its name at Bamford and Whatstandwell, and quite a contrast they are too. The former, Ye Derwent Hotel to give it its full title, is a high, twin-gabled building which was built around a century ago to catch the eye (if not the breath), while the latter is around 300 years old and is thought to mark the spot of a much earlier river crossing.

Predictably, the many and often age-old crossings of the River Derwent inevitably gave rise to hamlets and small communities, although sometimes the origins of names have become a little muddied. There was certainly once a ford at Whatstandwell between Cromford and Ambergate, and according to one tale it was a Walter Stonewell who lived at the house on the bank and built the originally fourteenth century bridge (hence the original name of 'Wattestanwell'). There again, others claim that a Walter Standwell was once a tollmaster and lived in part of the present building by the river. Either way, today's pub at Whatstandwell has stood for about three centuries and originally incorporated a toll house. It was once called the Bull's Head and served the coaches travelling the Derwent valley between Matlock and Derby.

Further upstream at Matlock, the Boat House Inn on Dale Road perhaps not surprisingly had a close association with the River

Derwent, given its name and the fact that it is just a few yards from the river. According to an ex-landlord, the 280-year-old pub has at various times also served as a mortuary and a brothel, a fact I have been unable to verify. However, the name definitely refers to the fact that row boats and pleasure craft were made in what is now the pub car park, since a foot ferry used to operate across the Derwent from this point.

At the Gate

'Gate' or 'gata' is an old Norse word for a road, and pubs and places of this name are still associated with many roads today. In terms of hostelries, rather than simply referring to any old field gate, it can sometimes mean a specific barrier – and not just for passing through, either. There are Gate Inns at Matlock and Tansley, plus three Hanging Gates.

The first of these is at Higher Sutton, near Langley, and is well worth seeking out, despite its rather remote location high on a quiet country lane in Cheshire (leave the A54 Buxton-Congleton road for the lane northwards to Sutton Lane Ends). The Hanging Gate perches on the side of Cophurst Edge and enjoys an altitude of almost 1,100ft (334m), and not surprisingly enjoys terrific views across the Cheshire countryside.

A welcome for travellers – the sign of the Hanging Gate near Chapel en le Frith.

It's been an inn since the 1600s, and is believed to be sited near the spot (the so-called Greenway Stone) where poachers and rustlers caught in the nearby Royal Macclesfield Forest were hanged. The McGrath family have run the charming pub, which occupies several levels and is a popular eating place, for over a decade. The favourite spot for diners is the small, west-facing dining room (known as 'the view room'), but in summer the terraced beer garden is also a great place to take in the panorama. If you visit in the colder months you'll no doubt enjoy the cosy lounge bar, with an open fire; or the tiny but elegant Blue Room.

But for the purists, the highlight is probably the traditional snug bar – dark and intimate, as it should be – where you can sup your pint of Hydes and enjoy a natter. No doubt the same bar has served a similar function for the last three centuries, with all manner of travellers passing through, including drovers and packhorse jaggers who are known to have used this route over the wild Cheshire moorland to the plains below.

Despite the rather grisly story behind the gate, the modern message for bona fide visitors on the sign outside is much more welcoming:

This gate hangs here
and troubles none
refresh and pay
and travel on.

A similar welcome exists at another Hanging Gate pub, this one located just outside Chapel en le Frith on the road to Whaley Bridge. It's already been mentioned in Chapter 2, since the location is known as Cockyard, which hints at what might have gone on at the pub in centuries gone by. Today it's a cosy and pleasant place, popular with families and dining groups at weekends, and its welcoming greeting inscribed on the pub sign (again, a wooden bar gate) is similar to the last: 'This gate hangs free and hinders none, refresh yourself and travel on'.

Ironically, the gate in question used to be a toll gate, so travellers would have little option but to stop at this point. A similar story is associated with the Ye Olde Gate at Brassington in the far south of the Peak District – see Chapter 5 on haunted pubs.

Small and perfectly formed

Since Peak pubs come in all shapes and sizes, there are plenty of smaller and more intimate establishments which are also worth seeking out. Many were once private dwellings, converted or knocked through to form a public house.

The Packhorse Inn at Little Longstone is typical. It began as a terraced row of two or possibly three miners' cottages, probably built some time in the 1600s and became a pub on August 4, 1787, when its owner was recorded as a miner and innkeeper. As its name suggests, the pub was probably a regular stopping point for trains of packhorses and traders heading over Longstone Moor. The rooms are small and cosy, simply but appropriately furnished, and every Wednesday evening they are the venue for a regular folk session when musicians come together to play.

Today the pub also hosts travellers not on four hoofs but two wheels, since it is located on the popular Monsal Trail, an eight-mile walking/cycling route which links Bakewell with Wyedale, near Buxton, and for much of the way follows the route of Midland Railway's former London-Manchester line.

Another pub associated with the jaggers and their packhorse trains is the Cheshire Cheese on the Edale Road at Hope, which like its Little Longstone equivalent can trace its pedigree back several centuries. It, too, boasts an open fire and good home-cooking, a wonderful combination on a cold winter's day, and for a traditional Peak District country inn, it is hard to beat. The building was originally a farm, built by the local Hall family in about 1660, and when it became a pub in the mid 1700s, it was originally called the Waggon and Horses. Later, two annual fairs were held here, when cattle and horses, and the likes of cheese and cloth, were sold.

The Star Inn at Tideswell has three tiny bars and a side room and is a fascinating little place, still very much a genuine locals' pub. The Thorn Tree Inn at Matlock is different again, located high up on the northern side of the valley among the town's residential back streets. It's on Jackson Road, which is off Smedley Street West, but although it's not the easiest pub to find it is definitely worth nosing out. The pub comprises two tiny bars – the 'smoke room' and 'public bar' – both of which are richly decorated by all manner of period memorabilia from the Edwardian and Victorian eras.

Another diminutive town pub, again well-preserved and protected from the excesses of modern refurbishment, is the Baker's Arms at Buxton. Originally believed to have had some connection with a bakery, it has a parlour bar and a snug that are sympathetically furnished in keeping with its history as a traditional town alehouse (rather than a coaching inn or hotel). Look out, incidentally, for the photos, scarves and other football mementoes, including souvenirs from overseas trips, associated with the pub's own football team.

A small and traditional pub, but from an earlier era, is the Old Bull's Head at Little Hucklow, a hamlet located off the Bradwell-Tideswell road. The building claims to date from the twelfth century, and although this is hard to substantiate there's no doubting it's an old, old place. The two diminutive bars are separated by great thick walls and huge oak beams, while upstairs is another small room called the Cave that is occasionally used by groups and for meetings. Previous innkeepers were also miners, and there was once a shaft in the pub's cellar that connected it with the mine below.

The Cliff Inn at Crich also shares a mining history, since the building was originally believed to have been built for the manager of the local quarry. Converted to a pub around 100 years ago, the two unpretentious bars are simply decorated, and handy for visits to the popular National Tramway Museum just up the road.

Connoisseurs of the pocket-sized rather than the pint-sized, as it were, might also like to visit the Church Inn at Darley Dale and the White Hart at Bradwell. The Goyt Inn, at Whaley Bridge, is a cosy one-bar pub on a side-street near the canal basin, while a couple of miles away the Swan Inn at Kettleshulme boasts two dark and atmospheric bars, with period seating, a grandfather clock and massive wooden beams.

Like the Packhorse Inn at Little Longstone, the Red Lion at Litton is made up of three old cottages knocked through, as is the Flying Childers at Stanton in Peak (both also have lovely open fires in the tap-rooms) and the Ship Inn at Wincle. The Princess Victoria occupies what is in effect a small shopfront on South Parade at Matlock Bath; while further south along the A6, approaching Whatstandwell, is the Homesford Cottage Inn.

It was originally built to serve the navvies who pioneered Midland Railway's line along the valley to Matlock, and despite its position on one of the main highways into the Peak District (its car park is across the other side of what can be a very busy road), the pub still retains a cosiness and approachability, plus a reputation for decent, home-cooked meals. Traditional Sunday lunch is still many people's favourite, apparently.

A question of style

It goes without saying that pub architecture varies according to location and background, from the modest village local or remote wayside hostelry to the showy urban taverns and grand coaching inns.

There are former manorial buildings, such as the Peacock Hotel at Rowsley (Chapter 4) with its stately, ivy-clad exterior and association with the landed gentry. The Norfolk Arms at Ringinglow, on Sheffield's western moors, dates from 1804 and was built in the same Gothic fashion as the octagonal toll house erected across the road around 20 years earlier. It has a splendid castellated frontage, with triangular-headed windows and tall, narrow chimneys. At the other end of the scale is the authentic, red-brick Navigation Inn at Buxworth (Chapter 3), a reminder of the industrial age.

At the Hope and Anchor in Wirksworth you have to go inside to admire its architectural claim to fame. The story goes that long before it became a town centre tavern the solid, three-storey building by the market place was originally the residence of a prison governor, because during the seventeenth century, Wirksworth housed a large number of convicts. And it is these French prisoners of war that are possibly thought to be responsible for the intricately-carved wooden chimney piece in the lounge bar of the pub, dating from around 1660, and which was originally the parlour of the house. In its centre is a pattern of four fleur-de-lis, flanked by two unicorns. At the bottom corners are what looks like Tudor roses. It's certainly an elaborate decoration in what is today just a small corner bar.

The original Hope and Anchor was further down the main street, and one of its more interesting features appears to have moved with it. As you walk through the grand main entrance of the present pub look up at the ceiling. There's a small but beautifully-designed stained glass window directly above, depicting a Pre-Raphaelite-looking woman (long hair, flowing robes, wistful expression) draped around an anchor.

If you walk around the corner on to Coldwell Street, past the Red Lion, you come to another pub with an interesting background. The Vaults was the former business premises of Charles Wright & Son, established around 200 years ago and an important wine and spirit merchants. At one time their operations included whisky-blending, and until it was demolished in the 1970s, there was a large warehouse to the back.

It's surprising what sometimes lurks inside other ostensibly unremarkable-looking pubs. For instance, the bar of the Waterloo Inn at Biggin boasts, rather unusually, an authentic Midland Railway bench which could once be found on Derby Railway Station. The interior of the Bowling Green at Ashbourne is decorated by masks and carvings from Africa and the Middle East, collected by the landlady on her travels around the globe.

Elsewhere, the collections are equally eclectic. The Bridge Inn at Calver is surely one the very few pubs in the land which boasts a collection of antique fire-fighting equipment, with unusual copper extinguishers and the like. A vast array of Toby jugs adorns the Angler's Rest at Miller's Dale; while bank notes from around the world are pinned to the ceiling at the George at Alstonefield.

The Cock and Pullet at Sheldon (see Chapter 8) is full of clocks, while Mary's Wine Bar at the Old Hall Hotel (Buxton) and the Barley Mow at Bonsall are crammed full of chicken memorabilia. The Fleece Inn at Holme, two miles south west of Holmfirth, has a display of pottery and local crafts; while the Friendship Inn on Arundel Street in Glossop has a fine collection of cricketing paintings and prints. But the Chequers Inn on Froggatt Edge goes one step further. The dining room is home to the 'Chequers Paintings', featuring changing displays and exhibitions by mainly local artists.

A few pubs still retain traditional snug bars, intimate little side or back rooms, most notably the Bell Inn at Cromford. The Devonshire Arms at Pilsley is also one of the very few true estate pubs left, owned (like most of the village) by the Chatsworth estate. The pub dates from 1739, and is fronted by four distinctive window gables and exceptionally high chimneys.

The neighbouring village of Edensor (pronounced 'Enzer') is also owned by the Chatsworth estate, and once sported a number of pubs and refreshment points for the large numbers of tourists that flocked to the stately home and its glorious grounds. They still come, of course, but at Edensor they have to make do with the Post Office tearooms. Incidentally, most of the original village of Edensor was allegedly moved from across the road after the Duke decided it marred his view from Chatsworth House. It was designed by Sir Joseph Paxton, head gardener to the 6th Duke of Devonshire (who was also responsible for the Crystal Palace).

He also had a hand in the layout of Beeley, an estate village at the southern end of Chatsworth, and that included the pub. Called, rather inevitably, the Devonshire Arms, it is an amalgam of three separate cottages, converted in 1747 and subsequently a popular coaching inn. It continues to ooze character 250 years later, and although still owned by the Duke, for the last century or so the pub has been leased from Chatsworth and is privately run. It's a popular place for meals and often booked up in advance at weekends; so instead of the usual evening meal why not pop down on a Sunday morning for their special 'Victorian Breakfast'?

The Devonshire Arms at both Beeley and Pilsley have changed little in their lifetime, but one or two pubs have undergone complete make-overs; and some have even been demolished and completely rebuilt. For this we have to thank, or perhaps blame, contemporary trends in building and design, and perhaps the starkest example is the Millstone

The Devonshire Arms at Pilsley belongs to the Chatsworth estate and reflects the local influence of the Cavendish family.

Inn above Hathersage, which incorporates no less than three different architectural styles.

It is perhaps more remarkable still when you see a photograph of the original inn, a traditional two-storey farmhouse which was believed to date as far back as the 1630s. It was first licensed in 1820 and run by a Thomas Wilkin, who like so many other publicans at that time continued to farm. The attractive, whitewashed building was established on the turnpike between Sheffield and Chapel-en-le-Frith, handily close to 'Surprise View' where travellers from Yorkshire are treated to a sudden and dramatic view across the valley. Sadly, the old building was knocked down in 1929 and replaced by the modern three-storey hotch-potch of mock Tudor, Georgian and Regency. A similar fate befell the Scotsman's Pack just down the road in Hathersage – see Chapter 2.

The Millstone Country Inn, as it styles itself these days, is certainly a friendly and welcoming place, and takes its name from the millstones which were quarried from above the Derwent valley and which are now used as the boundary stone symbol of the Peak District National Park. It's just that from the outside, the pub looks like it was designed by an eight-year-old let loose on the drawing board.

7

What's Inn a Name?

Beating a path to the door

It's estimated that among the 50,000 or so pubs in Great Britain there are as many as 20,000 different pub names, and they can tell us a great deal about the history and make-up of a specific area – everything from local trades and the economy through to leading local families and past political allegiances. The Peak District has its fair share of rural names and family connections, but like anywhere else, the familiar ones keep reappearing, plus some rather unusual and unique examples.

To discover the origin of the some of the oldest pub names, we inevitably have to go back to their founding by the Romans (although the term 'pub' wasn't actually coined until Victorian times). In Ancient Rome, the *tabernae* – from which the term 'tavern' is derived – would be symbolised by vine leaves hanging outside the door to show that they sold wine, hence the term 'a good wine needs no bush'.

In this country, vines were replaced by the more hardy ivy or an evergreen bush hanging from a pole, and this is still remembered by the name of the Hollybush Inn at Grangemill at the top of Via Gellia near Cromford, and on the western edge of the Peak District at Bollington in Cheshire. A bundle of barley was another obvious symbol that was displayed outside or above the door. Until recently, it was customary at the unveiling of a new pub for a cluster of greenery, called an ale garland, to be hung at the door.

Another pub sign around today that dates from the same era is the Chequers, and proof of this has been provided by excavations of the Roman town of *Herculeaneum*, buried by the eruption of Vesuvius in AD79. Chequered signs have been unearthed that were displayed outside wine shops and taverns, and in today's Peak District you can visit the Chequers Inn on the A625 at Froggatt, near Calver. Board games such as draughts and chess were popular in ancient Rome, and evidently widely played in taverns. However, the chequers symbol was also the emblem of money-lenders in medieval times.

Biblical references and saintly legends

Many early pubs had a religious or sometimes specific biblical subject as their name, such as the crossed keys (the emblem of St Peter, the keeper of the keys to Heaven) which still lives on at Chapel Milton, near Chapel-en-le-Frith, with the Cross Keys Inn. The Lamb (for instance, at Chinley Head, near Hayfield, and on the extreme eastern edge of the Peak at Holymoorside) is often a reference to Christ; and the origin of others like the Mitre and the Angel is also obvious.

In addition to the biblical names, there are also a couple of saints amid the pub names of the Peak District. The Crispin Inn at Great Longstone, north of Bakewell, takes its name from St Crispin, patron saint of cobblers, shoe-makers and leather-workers. Boot and shoe making was a traditional village craft in Longstone.

As with so many of the saints, there are numerous legends told about Crispin, and the English version tells how he was born in Canterbury to the queen of Logia (Kent). In an attempt to avoid persecution by the anti-Christian Romans, Crispin and his brothers dressed in everyday clothes and fled to nearby Faversham. In the middle of the night and with nowhere to stay, they heard music and song from behind a door, and knocking they asked whether they could come in. The house belonged to a master shoemaker named Robards, who took pity on them, and before you know it they all moved in and Crispin began a seven-year apprenticeship.

So good was their work that Robards found himself appointed shoe-maker to Roman Emperor Maximinus. Crispin was commanded to make shoes for Ursula, the Emperor's daughter, and while presenting them to her in Canterbury he was struck by her beauty and fell in love with her. They ended up marrying in secret, and when Maximinus discovered Crispin's high birth he eventually acquiesced to their marriage, saying: "A shoemaker's son is a prince born." Their wedding took place on October 25, since when it has become the Shoemakers' Feast Day.

It's a cracking good story, of course, and is the kind of thing you wouldn't put it past Disney turning into a soppy animated film. The real St Crispin and his brother, St Crispinian, were martyred in about AD287. They were Christians who fled persecution in Rome, and according to the stories provided the poor with shoes, taking no payment unless it was offered. Such was Crispin's benevolence that he even stole leather to make shoes for the poor.

St Crispin's Day is also the date of the Battle of Agincourt in 1415. The Crispin public house in Ashover, in the south east corner of the Peak District, reputedly gained its licence the year after Agincourt. A sign outside the pub explains how Thomas Babbington, Lord of the

Manor, and 'several men of Asher' returned victorious from the battle-field, and how they regarded St Crispin as their saviour.

Unfortunately there were less than saintly goings-on when Royalists troops were billeted in Ashover in 1646, as the sign also relates. They were there to patrol the Chesterfield to Matlock road, but according to eyewitness accounts the men were more interested in supping ale at the Crispin Inn. The landlord, Job Wall, blocked the doorway, telling them they had had quite enough already and they should be on their way. Unfortunately for him they 'turned him out and set watch at the door while the ale was drunk or wasted.'

Another saint has even stronger English credentials. Although pubs called the George usually refer to one of the English kings of that name, it is also associated with St George, and as at the lovely village pub at Alstonefield the sign depicts not a sombre monarch but the dragon-slaying saint.

The George and Dragon (in Ashbourne and Charlesworth, Glossop) is the more common pub name associated with this famous legend, of course, which saw George kill the dragon and save the life of the King's daughter, resulting in the heathen King converting to Christianity. Some time later, in the Crusades, it was reported that a vision of the saint appeared before the Christians during the siege of Antioch. Richard I immediately placed his army under the protection of St George, and went on to defeat the Saracens.

St Dunstan is also remembered in the Peak District, giving his name to a pub in Langley, near Macclesfield. Just as St Crispin has no known connection with Derbyshire, St Dunstan is unlikely to have visited this tiny Cheshire village. He began as a Benedictine monk at Glastonbury Abbey and went on to become Archbishop of Canterbury. Dunstan was notable for his artistic skills, such as painting and embroidery and working with precious metals. Today he is considered the patron saint of goldsmiths, as well as blind people and bell ringers.

By Royal Appointment

Although by the Middle Ages many inns and taverns had specific names, their signs were all important, since the majority of the population could not read. Pubs, like other traders and businesses, had to have easily-recognisable signs which were strong on visual imagery.

One of these was a white stag, which was a reference to King Richard II whose coat of arms featured a swan and an antelope with a collar. This became a white stag or hart on most signs. The story can be traced back to Alexander the Great, who is reputed to have caught a pure white stag and placed a gold collar around its neck.

It was in 1393, during Richard's reign, that pubs were ordered to display a sign so that they could be identified by the official ale taster (what a great job!). Not surprisingly, the white hart was immediately adopted by many establishments, and it soon became a generic term for a tavern in the Middle Ages. There are over 400 pubs of this name across the UK, and in the Peak District you can find White Hart Inns at Ashbourne, Bradwell, New Mills and Whaley Bridge.

Together with the church, the monarchy was the main influence on early pub names, and after Henry VIII split with Rome it is quite likely that a number of pubs (perhaps wisely) changed their name to demonstrate their loyalty to the monarch. Today there are still a huge number of pubs with royal connections, even though the face of the actual king or queen depicted on their signs tended to change with the fluctuating fortunes of the individual monarchs or royal houses.

The names which are still common today include general ones, such as the King's Head (Bonsall, Buxton), King's Arms (Chapel-en-le-Frith, Crich) and the Queen's Arms (Bakewell, New Mills, Taddington). Incidentally, this last name became something of a joke among former commercial travellers. When asked where they had stayed in a certain town, if they lived there and in fact had stayed at home they used to reply: "In the Queen's Arms".

In Bonsall, the sign for the King's Head (which usually commemorates Charles I, who of course famously lost his) appears to depict Charles II, which is a little odd. Perhaps it's more surprising, still, when you consider that the powerful Parliamentarian supporter John Gell lived not too far away at Hopton, near Wirksworth.

Mind you, Bonsall seemed to be a law unto itself, especially when you learn that at one stage there was even a Queen's Head to match the King's Head. The two pubs were next door to each other on the main square, and it is thought that, since there were stables behind the Queen's Head, perhaps the ostlers, coach drivers and servants used this pub, while the passengers stayed at the King's Head.

A couple of pubs are simply called the Royal: the handsome eighteenth-century hotel next to the River Sett at Hayfield in the High Peak; and the village pub at Dungworth, near Bradfield, in the far north east of the Peak District on the edge of Sheffield.

However, when it comes to the most popular pub names - in general - there are three that are out in front, and they all have royal origins: the

The Red Lion is one of the most common pub names in Britain, and this humorous sign is found at Birchover.

Crown, the Red Lion and the Royal Oak.

There are something in the region of 700 pubs across the UK called the Crown. Ironically, only a handful are located in the Peak District, including the modern Wetherspoon pub which overlooks Crown Square in the centre of Matlock, plus a Crown in Glossop and Ye Olde Crown in Waterhouses, Staffordshire.

The name was widespread, probably because the royal crown was a clear and unambiguous visual symbol, and of course represented loyalty to the monarchy in general rather than an allegiance to any one particular sovereign – a clear case of hedging your bets. As with other royal pub signs, it is believed that many made a swift and tactful change of name during England's short lived republic in the 1650s, but the fact that so many have survived to this day must surely be some sort of testimony to the country's enduring relationship with its monarchy. In the case of the Crown, the name was often given to a place after it received some sort of royal patronage, or if it stood on royal land.

There are plenty of pub names where the crown is crossed with something else. The ubiquitous Crown and Anchor, for instance, is the badge of the lord high admiral, and a favourite with retiring seamen who become innkeepers. The Rose and Crown, such as at Allgreave on the Buxton-Congleton road, clearly indicates loyalty to the mother country, but it also symbolised the end of the Wars of the Roses which had divided the nation for many years. The Crown and Mitre (near Chinley) represents the not always easy relationship between government and the Church; or was it another example of the publican being rather canny, I wonder?

The second most common pub name is the Red Lion, with over 650 throughout Britain. It symbolises the badge of John o' Gaunt, Duke of Lancaster (1340-99), although it also crops up in Scottish heraldry after James I (James VI of Scotland) ordered that it should be included on his coat of arms and displayed on all important public buildings (including pubs). It certainly is prolific in the Peak District, with Red Lions at Bakewell, Birchover, Hognaston, Kniveton, Litton, Matlock Green, Stone Edge, Thorncliffe, Wensley, Waterfall (Staffs) and Wirksworth.

Meanwhile, the less widespread White Lion dates from the time of Edward IV, and there are pubs of this name at Buxton, Disley, Great Longstone and Starkholmes, near Matlock. But, as with many heraldic pub signs, there is an alternative explanation, since a white lion also featured on the badge of the Duke of Norfolk who owned land in the Peak District. Likewise, the Black Lion can refer to Queen Philippa of Hainault, wife of Edward III; or alternatively to the fourteenth-century Welsh freedom-fighter Owain Glyndwr, Prince of Wales.

The third most popular pub name in Britain has a well-known royal connection, but you may have to cast your mind back to school history lessons in order to remember it. The Royal Oak commemorates the dramatic escape of Charles II after defeat at the Battle of Worcester in 1651, and at the last count there were as many as 540 dotted about England.

The name tells how the would-be monarch famously hid from his pursuers in an old oak tree (the Boscobel Oak) in Shropshire. Following the Restoration of the Monarchy, Charles II declared that 29th May, the King's birthday, should be celebrated as Royal Oak Day or Oak Apple Day. In the Peak District you can toast the moustachioed and be-wigged King in Royal Oaks at Chapel-en-le-Frith, Hayfield, Hurdlow, Millthorpe (in the Cordwell valley south west of Dronfield), New Mills, Tansley, Wigley (west of Chesterfield) and Wirksworth.

It's said that Royal Oak pubs were often run by Royalists, while King's Head pubs were frequently occupied by supporters of Parliament (because the King's head is what they wanted). Supporters of either side claimed they would not enter a pub which indicated support for the other.

The Rising Sun, suggesting a new dawn and a bright future, is depicted on the coat of arms of Edward III, William II and William III. There are Rising Sun pubs on the A6187 between Hope and Bamford, and above the crossroads at Middleton by Wirksworth.

The White Boar, emblem of Richard III, was a popular inn sign during his reign in the mid fifteenth century, and as C. Lamb points out in his guidebook to inn signs, these particular publicans must have thanked the Earl of Oxford, whose crest was a blue boar, for supporting Henry Tudor (who defeated Richard III at the Battle of Bosworth). "They had only to paint the boar blue to show a healthy respect for the new reign," he observes.

Clearly a knowledge of heraldry is useful when it comes to deciphering some royal pub signs, but luckily others are much more comprehensible. The Queen Anne at Great Hucklow appears to be named after the last Stuart monarch, who died in 1714, although records from 1851 show that it was formerly called the Queen's Head and the landlord went by the splendid name of Caleb Higinbottom.

A more recent and longer-reigning monarch is remembered in a pub name at Matlock Bath. The Princess Victoria on South Parade is a small and unostentatious little place whose name (note the Princess, not Queen) commemorates the visit to the resort of Victoria in 1832 before she reached the throne. There is no record of the pub, which used to be a shop, ever having the received the Queen-to-be, but since when have facts ever got in the way of a good story? The pub's friendly resident ghost is, rather inevitably, called Albert. Meanwhile, her Prince Consort is more properly remembered by the Albert Hotel at Disley; and further north, at Hadfield near Glossop, our longest-reigning monarch is also celebrated by the Victoria Inn.

Other royal figures featured in Peak pubs include the Duke of York, although of course there are a number of different ones. You can find

The George Hotel at Youlgrave is named after the English monarch, but exactly which one is uncertain since its sign appears to depict several possible candidates.

local examples at Buxton, Elton and Pomeroy, on the A515 near Flagg.

Another common royal pub name is the George, with pubs bearing this name at Glossop, Hathersage, Hayfield, Tideswell, Waterhouses and Youlgrave. Of course, there were several kings of that name, and at the George Hotel at Youlgrave they get round the problem of identification by depicting four separate Georges on the pub sign outside. The royal House of Hanover is also remembered in the White Horse, a Saxon motif, and in the Peak District there's one at Horwich End, near Whaley Bridge.

The Prince of Wales is located at Baslow, Buxton and Glossop, and usually they are named after Edward VII, who became King in 1901, although sometimes they can refer Edward II who held the title in the fourteenth century.

A military connection

Well-known military battles are also represented by pub names, with the Waterloo Hotel on the A6 near Taddington, and the Waterloo Inn at Biggin, north of Ashbourne. The famous victory of the Duke of Wellington against Napoleon in 1815 gave rise to numerous pubs bearing the name of this location in what is now Belgium; and of course it also paved the way for the victorious commander to be remembered in pub names the length of the country.

In the Peak District you can raise a glass to the Duke of Wellington at Matlock - the pub is located at the top of town where Chesterfield Road meets Wellington Street; and at the Wellington in Ashbourne (which changed its name from the Nag's Head to celebrate the beating of the French). In fact, the Iron Duke, who after his success went on to become foreign secretary and prime minister, appears in more English pub signs than any other military figure apart from Admiral Nelson. In the landlocked Peak District, the hero of Trafalgar is celebrated at the Nelson Arms at Middleton-by-Wirksworth.

Another naval man is celebrated by the name of the village pub at Onecote (pronounced 'Onkut') on the Staffordshire Moorlands. The Jervis Arms, standing by the young River Hamps, commemorates Admiral Jervis, whose name I am reliably informed is pronounced 'Jarvis'. He was born in Staffordshire in 1735, and helped the British fleet to victory over French and Spanish ships off Cape Vincent in 1797. He was one of Britain's top admirals, and even commanded the young Horatio Nelson.

However, it's not just the powerful few – those at the top – who are commemorated. On the Buxton Road in Furness Vale, near New Mills, is a pub called the Soldier Dick. The sign outside depicts a wounded soldier, bandaged and supported by a crutch. The story goes that, some time in the 1600s, the landlord took in an injured soldier (in some accounts a deserter) returning from a distant battle, and his wife nursed him back to health. The man stayed on and became a popular and colourful local character, taking up painting and recounting stirring and often bloodcurling tales of his adventures for the pub's customers. The name 'Soldier Dick' is also sometimes said to stand for Richard Cromwell, Oliver Cromwell's son.

Another interesting tale concerns John Manners, Marquis of Granby (1721-70). He was the eldest son of the third Duke of Rutland and was the distinguished Commander-in-Chief in Germany during the Seven Years' War, famed in particular for the way he led his cavalry against the French at the Battle of Warburg. At the Battle of Minden he was leading a charge when both his hat and wig flew off, but despite this he continued the assault with gusto, thus giving the English language the immortal phrase 'going for the enemy bald-headed'.

By all accounts he was a popular leader, once described as 'brave to a fault, skilful, generous to profuseness, careful to his men and beloved by them'. After his campaigns he rewarded his senior non-commissioned officers who had been injured or disabled with a gratuity for them to set themselves up as innkeepers, hence the enduring popularity of the pub name around the country today. Indeed, one epitaph for the Marquis Granby reads:

> *What conquest now will Britain boast,*
> *Or where displays her banners?*
> *Alas, in Granby she has lost*
> *True courage and good manners.*

There was once a Marquis of Granby pub in Ashbourne, but in recent times the sole survivor in the Peak District has been a handsome old hotel in the Hope Valley by the Bamford turning. Unfortunately it closed shortly before this book was written, and the premises are currently up for sale. Perhaps it is timely, therefore, to learn that John Manners (once the Lord Lieutenant of Derbyshire) died leaving debts of £37,000. He was painted a dozen times by Sir Joshua Reynolds, and most of the surviving pub signs are based on these portraits.

The Marquis of Granby at Bamford was particularly notable for its

Olympic Room, which was fitted out with decorative woodwork from the White Star liner *RMS Olympic*. She was the lesser-known sister ship of the *Titanic*, and after a long life during which she managed to successfully dodge icebergs and enemy bombs, she was broken up on the Clyde in the 1930s. Her luxurious interior fittings were then sold off, some of which found their way to the Marquis of Granby in Derbyshire. Sadly, it is understood that they have all been removed and sold.

Other pubs have their own story to tell, but like so many rooted far back in the past, it is not always easy to separate fact and fiction. The 400-year-old village pub at Grindon, a peaceful community high above the Manifold valley in Staffordshire, started off as the village smithy, was once called the Shoulder of Mutton, but at the some point the name was changed to the Cavalier. It was a term given to a Royalist who fought for King Charles I during the English Civil War, of course, and indeed the pub sign depicts a dapper and smiling fellow straight from that era.

However, some say that the new name was possibly bestowed in honour of Bonnie Prince Charlie, who is said to have stayed in the village during his march south from Scotland in the 1745 Rebellion. Other Peakland pubs that he or his followers are supposed to have stayed in include the Ship at Wincle, and the Royal Cottage on the Staffordshire moors (see Chapter 2).

Odd and unusual names

A highly distinctive pub name can be found in the Staffordshire hamlet of Sheen, perched on a low ridge separating the valleys of the Dove and Manifold near Hartington. The Staffordshire Knott takes its name from the county emblem (it's incorporated in the badge worn by the Staffordshire police force), and originated around 1400 with the Earls of Stafford. However, there's another tale suggesting that a former Sheriff of Stafford devised the triple knot as a means of hanging three men at once.

The Staffordshire Knots was also the nickname of the South Staffordshire Regiment, and the story of how they supposedly acquired this moniker is intriguing. The 38th Foot Regiment was sent to Antigua in 1706, but for several decades the War Office effectively forgot all about them. With no new uniforms sent out they were forced to patch their increasingly threadbare tunics with brown holland (a coarse linen cloth that took its name from the country where it originated). Thereafter it was customary to wear a piece of this cloth behind the cap badge to commemorate this period, which soon became known as the Staffordshire Knot.

Some pub names, like the Staffordshire Knott, you can perhaps guess at, but there are others that unless you have the benefit of some specialist knowledge can leave you totally bewildered. One such is the Grouse and Claret at Rowsley, the name of which you would think probably refers to a shooting party out on the moors above Chatsworth, and the prospect of some well-cooked game and a glass of red wine in the evening. This is reinforced by the presence of the Grouse Inn just a mile or so down the road in Darley Dale, whose sign clearly is of the plump, feathered game bird.

In fact, a grouse and claret is a type of artificial fly used by fly fishermen in the River Derwent, which flows through Chatsworth and Rowsley. Apparently it was a favourite of the local water bailiff. Glass cases mounted inside the pub have other examples of these expertly-created, look-alike flies, some of which are mentioned in relation to the nearby Peacock Hotel in Chapter 2.

The Peak District is blessed with its fair share of unusual and unique pub names. The Flying Childers is the village pub at Stanton in Peak, situated on the edge of Stanton Moor overlooking the Wye valley south east of Bakewell. It is a timeless, unspoilt two-room pub, converted several centuries ago from four cottages.

The Flying Childers at Stanton in Peak is named after a successful race-horse owned by the Duke of Devonshire.

Despite all the photographs of cricket teams in the bar, the pub takes its name from a champion racehorse from the 1720s and '30s, owned by the 4th Duke of Devonshire and trained by Sir Hugh Childers. He was said to be the first thoroughbred racehorse in England, sired by an import from Syria named Arabian. By all accounts the Flying Childers was a handsome animal, with a distinctive white flash, and he could also go like the clappers. He so daunted the opposition in his first race at Newmarket in 1721 that in his second race, six months later, all the other horses were withdrawn and he won in a walkover.

He was often known as the Devonshire Childers, after his owner, who refused several offers for the prize-winning animal, including one reputed to have been the equivalent weight of the horse in gold crowns. Flying Childers retired undefeated to the Duke's stud at nearby Chatsworth when his racing career ended. There is also another pub named after this racehorse at Kirby Bellars in Leicestershire.

Incidentally, Stanton in Peak was formerly the estate village of the Thornhill family, who still live at Stanton Hall; and the initials 'W.P.T.' which are carved into the stone above the pub's entrance stand for William Paul Thornhill.

An equally distinctive name (but, like the Flying Childers, not entirely unique) is the Quiet Woman at Earl Sterndale. The sign outside this unpretentious village pub, off the A515 south of Buxton, bears the picture of a decapitated woman with the motto: 'Soft words turneth away wrath.'

This unusual pub name and sign supposedly reflects the fate of the landlord's over-talkative wife.

There are several stories about its origin, but the one told the most often is of a former landlord who, returning from market at nearby Longnor and fed up with his wife's constant nagging, decided to have a quiet woman outside if he couldn't have one in. She is said to have had the nickname 'Chattering Charteris', and the tale relates how he chopped off her head after she wouldn't stop talking. But rather than condemn the landlord's actions, the other villagers were said to have had a collection to buy her a headstone and given what remained to the husband.

There are other examples of this pub name around the country, often with variations such as Silent Woman - one such used to exist in Calver in the Derwent valley. Another version is the Headless Woman, which can be found at Duddon, near Tarporley in Cheshire, and all allude to what may happen to over-talkative women. As the old rhyme goes:

> *Here is a woman who has lost her head*
> *She's quiet now – you see, she's dead.*

Eric Delderfield, author of a series of seminal books in the 1960s and '70s on the history of British pub signs, believes that this notable pub name may have originated during the reign of Henry VIII and referred, of course, to the beheading of Anne Boleyn.

Another Quiet Woman used to stand on the southern edge of Beeley Moor, a bleak expanse of upland high above the Derwent Valley east of Darley Dale. The pub was located on Flash Lane in the middle of the unpopulated moorland, and although it is now partly surrounded by newly-planted woodland, it's not hard to imagine what an unwelcoming and dangerous place it could be for passing travellers.

Of course, it doesn't help matters if the pub landlady goes in for a spot of robbery herself, for according to one report in this case she not only relieved them of their valuables but also polished some of her customers off and then buried them under the cellar floor. She was eventually arrested and hanged for her crimes, but not surprisingly the premises retained a sinister air and appeared to be plagued by mysterious goings-on, including unexplained fires.

The last pub buildings here were believed to have been erected in 1874 after a fire, and even when it was turned into a farm the problems persisted. As recently as 1966 a country club built on the site went up in flames, and when the owner began to rebuild the premises his temporary caravan located on the site was destroyed by fire.

Another account, related in Clarence Daniel's *Ghosts of Derbyshire* and which apparently goes back to Elizabethan times, tells how the moorland inn was in fact haunted by a female ghost with a reputation for arson. She was the surly and ill-tempered daughter of the landlord, who unwittingly drove her father to burn down the pub - unfortunately with him inside it. The tragedy left her unhinged and she was found dead on the moors some time later.

Now, if you think this is a little eerie, consider once again the other Quiet Woman. Half a century ago, the church at Earl Sterndale had the dubious distinction of being the only one in the whole of Derbyshire to be bombed during the Second World War. In June 1941 a German plane believed to be returning from a raid on Manchester dumped its incendiary bombs over the village and scored a direct hit on the church.

According to eyewitness accounts, the menfolk emptied out of the Quiet Woman opposite and rushed over to extinguish the flames, but such was the ferocity of the fire that the roof was completely burnt down, all the windows smashed and even the Saxon font broken. Miraculously, though, most of the walls remained standing, and a wedding booked for 11am the next day between William Wain and Annie Harrison actually went ahead in the open and gutted building. Perhaps the Quiet Woman was having her say after all?

Interestingly, a wartime bomb just missed the next pub with an unusual name. One night towards the end of the Second World War, fire-watchers on Axe Edge above the Goyt Valley had a narrow escape when an enemy flying bomb passed close above their heads. It landed just beyond the Cat and Fiddle Inn with a mighty explosion, and a crater is still visible in the ground.

But let's return to names. On the face of it, the Cat and Fiddle presents a much more straightforward example, but in fact here again there are various accounts of its origin. The fire-watchers, huddling on the moors 50 years ago, were there for a reason, for the pub sits 1,690 ft (515m) high up on a breezy ridge mid-way between Buxton and Macclesfield on the A537 and enjoys spectacular views. For everyone from map-makers to holidaymakers, location and pub name are synonymous, and for motorists in particular the winding and sometimes treacherous road can be notorious.

Hey diddle diddle... an eye-catching stone relief by the entrance of the Cat and Fiddle pub high up on the Cheshire moors.

As for the derivation of the name, the obvious answer is that it comes from the popular nursery rhyme ('Hey diddle diddle, the cat and the fiddle...') which first appeared in popular culture as far back as the sixteenth or seventeenth centuries. However, another version suggests that the name was introduced in the 1850s after the Duke of Devonshire presented the landlord with a picture of a cat playing a violin. A sculptured relief still sits in the wall by the main porch. More intriguing, still, is another suggestion that the name stretches back to the Middle Ages and has some distant connection with Caton de Fidele, the governor of the English-held town of Calais.

The Bull i' th' Thorn on the A515 The pub supposedly dates from 1472, and replaced an original farmstead that had stood since the twelfth century. Determining the precise age of such places is not altogether easy; but there again perhaps it's not altogether important. It certainly *feels* like an incredibly old pub, a point reinforced by its oak panelling, stuffed bear, open fire and candle-lit banqueting room. As to the name, an oak carving said to date from the fifteenth century shows a bull tangled up in a thorn bush, and for once the explanation seems as straightforward as that.

All at sea in the Peak

For a region entirely landlocked like the Peak, it might come as a surprise that there are several pubs bearing nautical names. The Anchor Inn, on the A623 above Tideswell and at Hadfield, near Glossop, seems as far adrift from the ocean as you could possibly get in England, but originally the anchor in question did not necessarily belong to a ship.

Of course, there were plenty of ex-mariners who retired to take up innkeeping (see the earlier reference to the common name Crown and Anchor), and of course an anchor, like a crown, was a strong but simple

Although miles from the sea, the Ship Inn at Wincle is named after Shackleton's Antarctic expedition.

visual symbol. But there was another meaning attached to the anchor, stemming from the words of St Paul (Hebrews 6:19): "We have this as a sure and steadfast anchor of the soul..." A boat's spare anchor was often known as the (last) hope anchor; and the colour blue was regarded as the emblematic anchor of hope. Hence there are many pubs called the Blue Anchor or Hope and Anchor; and the latter overlooks the market square in Wirksworth.

The origin of the Ship Inn's name at Wincle is much more straightforward. This delightful country pub, situated in a peaceful hamlet on the Cheshire edge of the Peak District east of Congleton, dates from the sixteenth century and was created when three small cottages were knocked into one.

It was renamed early in the twentieth century in honour of Ernest Shackleton's successful expedition to the Antarctic, because his team included Sir Philip Lee Brocklehurst of nearby Swythamley Hall. The expedition's ship, a small whaler called *Nimrod*, is depicted stuck in the ice on one side of the pub sign, while the coat of arms of the Brocklehurst family is on the other. When he returned from the expedition Sir Philip received a medal from the Royal Geographic Society, and later served in the Life Guards during the First World War and commanded the Second Regiment of the Arab Legion during the Second World War.

Another story has it that a ship-builder friend of the Brocklehursts named a new ship *Swythamley*, after their family home, but the sailors had such trouble pronouncing the name they re-Christened her 'the Sweet Emily'.

The Animal World

The Greyhound Inn at Warslow, a former estate village near the Manifold valley, is a 250-year-old coaching inn which still provides a warm welcome for today's visitors. According to one account, the name refers to a local stagecoach (there was a famous one of the same name which used to run between London and Birmingham); but since the pub used to be called the Greyhound and Hare, perhaps the name has more to do with hare coursing?

Other animals which feature in Peak District pub names include, as we have already seen, the Lamb at Chinley Head and at Holymoorside and the Bear at Alderwasley, and you could once visit a Squirrel at New Mills. There's a muster of Peacocks (Bakewell, Owler Bar and Rowsley), a small herd of Packhorses (including Crowdecote, Little Longstone and

New Mills) and a Roebuck at Chapel-en-le-Frith. The Swan (Buxton, Kettleshulme, Marsden and New Mills) can also come either White (Ashbourne) or Black (Ashover, Crich); and of course there are various farmyard animals such as horses (nags), bulls and rams.

However, like royal pub names, some animal references can be misleading. Although there are around 450 pubs in Britain called the Swan, for instance, quite a few reflect an heraldic significance rather than a landlord's ornithological preferences.

A unique name is the Setter Dog, a pub high on the moors east of Macclesfield which sadly closed a couple of years before this book was written. It stood on the Buxton to Macclesfield turnpike and according to folklore was a popular haunt of highwaymen. As Louis McMeeken suggests in his book on place names of the Peak District, the name of the pub may refer to the slang term for a lookout, or the highwayman's accomplice who would keep an eye open for approaching coaches.

As mentioned earlier, the White Lion is usually a name associated with Edward V, but plenty of motorists are taken aback by the sign to the pub of this name on the main road through Disley. In what must be one of the most tongue-in-cheek pub signs in the Peak District, the painting actually depicts a zebra!

The only one of its kind?

Finally, a clutch of very unusual and perhaps unique pubs names, one of which still defies a convincing explanation. The pub in question is the Flouch Inn, situated in the north east corner of the Peak District between Langsett and Hazlehead. It was opened in 1827 as the New Inn, but why or when it was renamed, and what 'flouch' actually means, has left everyone mystified. The most common suggestion is that it refers to a speech impediment suffered by the first landlord, since a 'flouch lip' was said to be a slang term for a speech defect. Another, rather more simple explanation, is that the pub may have once been called the Plough and the letters fell off or got twisted.

Alongside the sensibly-named Black Swan, Cliff Inn and King's Arms at Crich, is a pub called the Jovial Dutchman. It was once a thatched building, but was largely rebuilt in 1904, and is said to take its name from a Dutch engineer who, like many of his fellow countrymen, came to Derbyshire to work on the Cromford Canal in the Derwent valley below (although some believe he may have been employed to drain the lead mines).

The canal was connected to the quarry at the top of the hill by a light railway, so no doubt some of the workforce stayed in Crich, including this particular fellow who became the pub's first landlord. A variation on the theme is provided by the pub name the Flying Dutchman, named after a famous racehorse, and found today at pubs at Wombwell, near Barnsley, and in Norwich.

Another unique name in the Peak is the Druid Inn, an attractive ivy-covered building in the village of Birchover, five miles south east of Bakewell. I have read that it's named after the Druids, a quasi-religious group who once worshipped on Rowtor Rocks behind the inn.

What is more certain is that the gritstone outcrop, half hidden among trees, is reachable via a small path which, together with a series of steps, seats and caves, was carved into the stone around 300 years ago under the direction of the Rev. Thomas Eyre of Rowtor Hall. It is said that he sat up there, high among the rocks, composing his sermons which he later delivered in the small church below.

As if to compound the vague sense of mysticism, above the village is an open area of heather and silver birch called Stanton Moor, dotted with various Bronze Age burial mounds and tumuli, and a stone circle called Nine Ladies. According to local legend shared with many other stone circles, these nine stone stumps are the remains of local women who were turned to stone while dancing on the Sabbath, while a separate stone – the King Stone – is all that remains of the fiddler who accompanied them.

The Knockerdown Inn, near Carsington Water on the southern edge of the Peak District, was formerly known as the Greyhound Inn. However, its change of name reflects an old nineteenth-century Derbyshire term 'knock-a-down', meaning a group of dilapidated buildings. It's now well-established as a popular family dining pub (see Chapter 8). Other unusual names include the Friendship Inn, an unassuming but welcoming corner pub on the back streets of Glossop; the Mousetrap Inn in Disley; and Ye Olde Mustard Pot in Midhopestones.

The story behind the Wanted Inn's name is particularly unusual. The pub is located at Sparrowpit, a small community on the A623 east of Chapel-en-le-Frith. Originally called the Three Tuns, it changed its name to the Devonshire Arms in 1839 to reflect its new owner. But when the 10th Duke tried to sell it in 1956 there were no takers, since it is, after all, in quite a remote and isolated spot. Two years went by with hardly any interest and not a single bid, and when new owners eventually took it over the pub was renamed the Wanted Inn – "the pub that nobody wanted."

The name game

A common if rather unimaginative pub name is the New Inn. It was usually given to a pub that replaced an older establishment, and it is estimated there are over 370 New Inns around the UK. Of course, plenty of these New Inns are themselves quite old and historic.

There are pubs of this name at Chapel en le Frith and in the village of Flash, high on the Staffordshire moors south of Buxton. The village claims it is in fact the highest in England, standing 1,518ft above sea level, and if you visit in anything other than the summer months you might well appreciate the welcoming log fire of the attractive seventeenth century village local.

Squeezed in between other buildings, the Black's Head overlooks Wirksworth's market place.

In these days of political correctness, the Black's Head at Wirksworth may not sit so easily in our lists when it comes to names, but who are we to try and amend authentic historical detail? A similar name can be found at Ashbourne, where the Blackamoor's Head was incorporated into the Green Man Royal Hotel when the two establishments merged many years ago (the famous gallows sign across the road still depicts a black man's face).

It's thought that, as at Wirksworth, the name may refer to an unfortunate victim of the slave trade; or possibly to a servant boy brought back from new territories abroad. More likely still is that it is a variation on the ancient inn name the Turk's Head or Saracen's Head, and refers to the times of the Crusades, when anyone of a darker skin was considered an infidel and unholy.

A few years ago, someone complained that the 'Black's Head' part of the Ashbourne hotel name and sign was a symbol of racial discrimination, and suggested that both the name and sign should be changed. The complaint, incidentally, did not come from an Ashbourne resident, and fortunately heritage won out and both are still in place.

Although it is said to be unlucky to change the name of a pub, this hasn't stopped countless places trying to switch their identity over the years. Often it is at the whim of a new owner, and some of the changes have certainly *not* been for the better.

By and large, the Peak District has resisted the trend – mostly urban, it has to be said – which in recent years has seen an influx of new and supposedly tongue-in-cheek names like the Slug and Lettuce and Brahms and Liszt. Glossop currently has a pub called the Last Orders, and for a while Monyash residents had to put up with the name of their local, the Bull's Head (one of the most authentic English pub names, of course), somewhat bizarrely being changed to The Hobbit.

What connection a diminutive character from Middle Earth has with a Derbyshire lead mining village is unclear, but the Tolkien theme was echoed at the former Royal Oak at Eyam that for a while in the 1980s was renamed the Prancing Pony, after the fictitious inn from *Lord of the Rings*. Not surprisingly, this went down badly with the locals, who promptly nicknamed the pub the 'Bonking Donkey'.

Another Bull's Head, this time at Foolow, became the Lazy Landlord for a time in the 1990s, and the equally historic Ram's Head at Disley was briefly the Hungry Horse, but fortunately both have gone back to their roots. The Lazy Trout at Meerbrook was probably not its original name; and according to one (admittedly unconfirmed) account, a pub in Longnor once had its name changed to the Train Robbers Den by a new landlord keen to display his collection of dodgy mementoes. It didn't last long.

The Waltzing Weasel at Birch Vale, between Hayfield and New Mills, would seem to be a name more in keeping with a city centre student bar. For 200 years the Waltzing Weasel was called the Birch Hall Inn, but its name change was not as recent as you might think.

You have to go back to 1965 to find the then landlady telling the local magistrates why she thought the name should be altered: "It sounds more rural in character," she said, "it has more scientific foundation, and it's a far more entertaining title than the present Birch Hall Inn!" The "scientific foundation" she mentions refers to the way in which weasels mesmerise their prey by appearing to dance or gyrate around them. In fact, there is also a pub in Manchester called the Dancing Weasel.

Most pub names appear to be changed by impulsive new landlords, or some distant marketing director of a faceless national pub or hotel chain. In most cases if they consulted the actual punters – the regulars – the answers might surprise them.

In 2003 the new landlord of the Queen's Arms at Taddington, Nathan Gale, decided to revert to the original name of the Miner's Arms. It had been renamed the Queen's Arms to celebrate Queen Victoria's Golden Jubilee in 1887.

To his credit, he put the name change to a referendum of Taddington residents, sending out voting slips to everyone in the village and also giving them out to customers (250 were handed out across the bar alone). "Is the Queen's Arm's name old and tired or is it still young and fresh?" he was quoted as asking in a local newspaper. "Instead of imposing a change, I thought I'd ask the villagers what they think."

Around two thirds of them rejected the original name in favour of the Queen's Arms. "I'm pleased that so many people were kind enough to vote," the landlord said afterwards. "We now have a corporate identity and can forge ahead with that." Unfortunately he left not long after, when his application to establish a brewery at the pub was rejected by the planning authorities.

8

Past and Present

Lost to history

Whether you're a pub aficionado or simply someone who enjoys an occasional trip to their local, it's a sad but inescapable fact that pubs and inns are no different to any other commercial activity. For most landlords and landladies the pub is a business, and in the case of national chains it is often run on strict business lines where the whims of the market place can count for much.

Inevitably, pubs come and go (usually go, it must be said), and one or two may even have altered or disappeared since this book was written. Long gone are the days when comparatively small villages like Winster could boast over 20 pubs and alehouses.

Mostly this reflects the decline in traditional industries and occupations like lead mining, but it's also a reflection of changing social patterns which began 150 years ago with a reaction against soaring levels of alcoholism and the unchecked proliferation of pubs and beerhouses. Lately pubs have had to compete against the growth of home entertainment, which is why village cinemas and picture houses have also largely vanished, as well as cheap alcohol from shops and supermarkets.

Many of the pubs in the Peak District, especially at the honeypot tourist sites, rely heavily on the spending power of visitors. The Peak District National Park is the second most visited in the entire world, so not surprisingly tourists provide a vital boost to the income of rural pubs and hotels. Indeed, it's almost certainly the case that many pubs in our region have been kept going through the money generated from the provision of meals and accommodation.

Despite that, there are plenty of inns and pubs that have been consigned to the great brewery in the sky, and while some of them are centuries old, there are others that have disappeared far more recently – and for a variety of reasons. The following is by no means an exhaustive list, and there are some in the larger towns and around the fringe of the Peak District which have not been included.

We begin our sorry stagger in the south of the Peak District at **Alstonefield**, where the Red Lion became Finderne House in the 1830s, and it is thought that the Black Lion could have become the village workhouse around the same time. Nothing remains of another village inn, the Harpur's Arms, although in nearby Longnor, the well-known South Derbyshire family is still remembered by the Harpur and Crewe Arms.

A shop in **Hartington**, between Dig Street and Hide Lane, was also once a pub called the Volunteer Arms, but in 1839 three people were killed when a barrel of gunpowder exploded in the rear of the premises. The George and Dragon at **Brassington** closed in the 1920s, and was divided into two properties: Dragon House and Dragon Cottage.

Kirk Ireton lost the Bull's Head, while at **Hognaston**, near Carsington Water, former pubs include the Pack Horse (believed to be present-day Stanbridge House or possibly Well House) and the Bull's Head. The latter was closed in the 1880s, and it is said that landlord, Samuel Hardy, closed the premises after a fight in the bar during which he was hit by a bottle, receiving cuts. Furious, he proceeded to open all the beer barrels and pour the demon drink away!

The historic market town of **Ashbourne** is said to have had as many as 36 named inns and pubs in Victorian times, as well as a fluctuating number of alehouses. They included the White Lion, Hare and Hounds, White Horse, Royal Oak, King's Head, Steam Engine (or Tailor's Arms), Red Lion, Barley Mow, Horse and Jockey, and Marquis of Granby – to name but a few. Among the more unusually-named former pubs were the Tiger, near the Vaults off the Market Place, the Ostrich (or Gaping Goose), and the Old Bear on Church Street; while the Talbot Inn was replaced by the Market Hall in 1850s.

On the steep, eastern side of the Derwent valley south of Cromford, the village of **Crich** has three surviving pubs, but in the mid nineteenth century, it supported 11 inns and 13 alehouses. The Wheatsheaf once stood at the top of Wheatsheaf Lane, and it is said that George Stephenson stayed here while working on the construction of the mineral railway between Ambergate and Cliff Quarry. The Greyhound could once be found in Roe's Lane, while the White Swan was located on the Market Place and was supposedly linked to the (existing) Black Swan by an underground passage. The Royal Oak and the Blue Bell (now Church Farm) have both gone, as has the Bull's Head (in 1954), plus the Shoulder of Mutton and Rising Sun (both in the 1970s). Records have also been found of a pub called the Last Drink Out near Causeway Lane.

At **Ashover** you could once sup at the White Lion, Yew Tree, Hand and Shears, Boot and Slipper, and Packhorse Inn. Most had gone long before 1900. The Junction Inn is recorded to have been in existence for about 40 years at **Lea Mills**, and was owned by the Arkwright family. It was located at High Peak Junction, where the Cromford and High Peak Railway met the Cromford Canal. The pub was reported to stand on a narrow strip of land between the canal and the railway, and it was demolished when the Midland Railway decided to straighten the track.,

Some years ago the Excavator Inn at Buckland Hollow, **Ambergate**, had a JCB (a real-life excavator) on its roof, but sadly – or perhaps fortunately – this was removed and the pub sign now celebrates another kind of excavator – the archaeologist.

A curious pub that existed a century ago in **Matlock** was the Hole in the Wall. It was located on Jackson Road, near the Friends' Meeting House, and there is speculation that its unusual name came from the activities of some of its rather shady customers. It has been suggested that the pub was used for selling on stolen goods, perhaps hidden in a hole in a wall; while a different tale links the pub to the so-called 'Great Matlock Will Case' of the 1860s. It concerned a will involving a piece of land off Snitterton Road that was challenged by three codicils, one of which was supposedly found in 'a hole in the wall'.

Beyond Matlock is **Tansley**, where today's Tavern at Tansley used to be called the George and Dragon. To local people it was known as the "Big Dragon", and the nearby Royal Oak was the "Small Dragon". An alehouse called the Dyers Arms, on South View, is believed to have closed around the 1850s.

Over to the south west of the Peak on the Staffordshire Moorlands, you could once find the Butcher's Arms (now Newhouse Farm) and the Dog and Partridge (now Moorland House) at **Onecote**. There is mention of the Royal Arms at nearby **Butterton**; and the Red Bull Inn was once a colourful hostelry in the centre of **Longnor** (at a time when there were as many as eight licensed alehouses in the village), but is now a private gallery.

In **Wirksworth**, the Crown Inn used to be found on the Market Place opposite the Hope and Anchor. It was a coaching inn first mentioned in 1758, but closed around 1910. The Green Man and the Three Tuns once stood on West End, while the Rose and Crown public house closed in 1876.

At nearby **Wirksworth Moor**, the Noah's Ark Inn shut up shop in 1918; while at the small mining community of Bolehill there were once four hostelries. Apart from the Miner's Standard, already mentioned in Chapter 3, you could once get a drink at the Hollybush Inn (now the location for the stables of Bolehill House), the New Inn (next to Bage Mine), and the Railway Inn. At **Parwich** you could once sup at the Crown and the Wheatsheaf, both long since vanished.

In the same area lies **Bonsall**, another village steeped in mining history, and according to research by Peter Fellows as part of the Bonsall History Project, there were once as many as 12 pubs in or close to the parish, including nine actually in the small village. Today only the King's Head and Barley Mow remain, but as we have seen in the previous chapter, the Queen's Head used to stand next to the King's Head; and the names of both the Miner's Standard (in the High Street) and Pig o'Lead at the Via Gellia junction (which closed in 1995) recall the days of lead mining.

Another High Street pub was the Britannia Inn, which closed at the end of the nineteenth century; and Briars Inn, off Black Tor Road, is now known as Briars Inn Farmhouse. The New Inn, on Yeoman Street, was renamed the Fountain, and finally closed in 1983. There are believed to have been several pubs up on the moors above Bonsall, including the Gate Inn at Slaley, but little or no records exist.

At the top of Via Gellia is **Grangemill**, where in addition to the surviving Holly Bush Inn there was a second called the Lillies Inn. It was named after the plant that was once plentiful in the valley; but the pub closed in 1956 and has since become a private house.

On the other side of Slaley Moor lies **Winster**, which in 1750 had two dozen inns and alehouses. Long-lost venues include the Bull's Head (East Bank), the Crown (Main Street), Shoulder of Mutton (West Bank), and also the Wheatsheaf. A pub or alehouse called the Derbyshire Sally came to a conclusive end in 1785, when it was blown up after an accident thought to involve mining explosives.

Winster Hall became a pub in 1984, after operating as a B&B, but then after changing hands several times it reverted to a private residence. The original pub sign depicted a group of Morris dancers which was styled on a photograph of the famous local Winster Morris men. Another well-known inn was the Angel, opposite the Old Hall, and both this and Winster Hall were reputedly haunted – see Chapter 5 for the full stories.

Just along from Winster is the village of **Wensley**, which waved goodbye to the Crown in 1997; while heading back northwards, to the present-day B5056, you could once knock back a pint at the Piper Inn until it fell derelict in the 1930s. Turning right at Grangemill, on to the A5012, Pikehall Farm at the hamlet of **Pikehall** was formerly the

Pikeham Inne, once a well known roadside stop for travellers.

Back along the same road at **Cromford**, pubs that have long vanished include the Bull's Head, which stood by the Market Place at the end of Scarthin until it was demolished in the late 1800s. The Cock Inn was situated on North Street (Cromford Hill), opposite the Bell Inn, which is still there. Further down the hill stood the Crown, which became a butchers and ended up a private residence. At the very top of the long slope was the Cromford and High Peak Railway Inn, which not surprisingly became shortened to the Railway Inn.

The King's Head, described as a three-storey Georgian inn, once stood next to Masson Mill and served as the manager's residence; while the Rutland Arms was built for the workers in 1842 in a terraced row directly opposite the mill. Both the King's Head and the Rutland Arms were demolished in the 1970s to allow the A6 to be widened.

A pub called the Thorn Tree existed in the mid 1800s in **Birchover**; while **Youlgrave** once had a fourth pub, the Thornhill Arms, situated opposite the church a couple of doors down from the George Hotel.

The small communities either side of 'Pommy' – to give Youlgrave its local nickname – could also once boast their own watering holes. The Bateman Arms at **Middleton-by-Youlgrave**, located in Square House overlooking the main square, was named after the famous Victorian antiquarian and pioneering archaeologist Thomas Bateman who lived at Lomberdale Hall near the village. The original sign is now in the village hall.

Heading eastwards you come to the hamlet of **Alport**, most of which is tied to the Duke of Rutland's Haddon estate. However, the village also marks the confluence of the Rivers Bradford and Lathkill, and the mile or so that they run together down to the River Wye near Haddon Hall is still known to one or two older residents as the River Daykin.

I have seen an extremely old image of a pub called the Three Rivers Inn which once stood by the road bridge across the Lathkill at **Alport**. In more recent times the Boarding House Hotel occupied a similar site (perhaps the same?) on Alport Hill, but this was demolished just before the Second World War when the road was straightened to make it safer. Today **Monyash** is left with just a solitary pub, the Bull's Head, but at one time there were as many as five, including the Golden Lion and Bay Horse.

However, it comes as no surprise today to find that **Bakewell**, with its annual influx of visitors, still supports six pubs, a large hotel and several bars. But the list of former inns and taverns is even more extensive, as research by the Bakewell and District Historical Society has shown. The background to the Rutland Arms Hotel, which was built on the site of the White Horse Inn, has already been mentioned in Chapter 6; but in addition to this there were plenty more small pubs and alehouses dotted around the town.

The Flying Childers was used as a beerhouse during the construction of the railway - it occupied a signalman's house close to Bakewell Station – and nearby was the Station Hotel. On Matlock Street you could once find the Nag's Head and Todd's Vaults, and on Mill Street stood Britain's Pride (it became Skidmore's grocers) and the White Swan. Near here was the Crown (later the King's Arms) and the New Inn, the latter built by mill-owner Richard Arkwright.

On Bagshawe Hill was the Union Hotel, while on Monyash Road you could find the Staffordshire Arms and Sheldon Lane End, and at the junction with Yeld Road stood the Royal Standard. The Anchor Inn was knocked into the present-day Wheatsheaf, and until the early 1900s the Angel Inn was located at the corner of Water Street and Water Lane.

Close to the historic Market Hall was the Durham Ox, presumably a favourite with traders; while the Pineapple Inn, off Baslow Road, was a popular haunt of the men working on the construction of the adjacent new Midland railway line, now the Monsal Trail.

Following the Wye downstream to its junction with the Derwent at **Rowsley**, we pass the site of the village's two former inns – the Nag's Head and Red Lion. South from here is **Darley Dale,** or more accurately **Two Dales**, where the Blacksmith's Inn (now a private house) and the Nag's Head (demolished) once stood.

To the north we enter the grounds of Chatsworth and come to **Edensor**. Originally there were as many as eight pubs or ale outlets, including the Edensor Inn, now the Chatsworth Institute. Boswell visited it in 1775 not long after it had opened and reported that it had a "very jolly landlord". The neighbouring estate village of **Pilsley** once boasted the Snake and Crown, which is clearly a reference to the Duke's family crest (see Chapter 4). At **Calver** you could once find the Bull's Head next to the three-storied London Tavern (later the Co-op) as well as the Silent Woman, Miner's Arms, and Drum and Monkey.

Taddington, high on the central White Peak plateau, has traditionally been a popular place for travellers to seek rest (or shelter), since it's located on one of the principal east-west routes across the region. There were once six inns or alehouses in the village, including the George Hotel, first opened in the 1750s and later turned into flats. The Bull's

Head is believed to have stood opposite the present-day Queen's Arms, while the Star Inn (now Star House) was located at the western end of the village next to the church, and for some time it incorporated part of the village's historic Norman font which was used to wash dirty beer mugs. The font was finally returned to the church in 1939.

The Miner's Arms dates back to 1736, and at one time its cellar was used as a makeshift morgue, since the local coffin-maker lived across the street. In 1887 the pub changed its name to the Queen's Arms, and we have already seen what happened when the new landlord tried to change it back a century later (Chapter 7). Elsewhere, a beerhouse called the Traveller's Rest which opened around the 1850s later became the Marlborough Temperance Hotel (see Chapter 5), and in more modern times ended up as Marlborough House, offering bed and breakfast.

You could once lean against the bar at the Hare and Hounds in **Litton**, while at **Tideswell** the Cross Daggers Inn burned down in 1937 and the site is now occupied by the Ex-Servicemen's Club. The Three Tuns Inn (the name was from the crest of the Vintners Company) could once be found on the Market Place, but is now a private dwelling.

Nearby was the Belle Vue Hotel, later renamed the First Drop Inn. It had a dining room named the Drunken Butcher in honour of William Bennett, a local poet. A ballad relates the story of a Tideswell butcher who, after a having a few too many to drink at Sparrowpit, was supposedly chased all the way home over the moors by a ghost.

You could once buy a round at the Miner's Arms on Church Street; while near the church gates was the Bull's Head and King's Head (demolished in the late 1950s). Finally, the Peacock Hotel closed in the 1970s after Freddie and Connie Lomas Fletcher, tenants for 36 years, decided to retire. Interestingly, like at Matlock, there was once a pub called the Hole-in-the-Wall. It was approached via steps from the Market Place, and apparently acquired its name from its tiny entrance. The open space behind the building was once used for cock fighting and bear baiting.

Out to the west, in Cheshire, you could once drown your sorrows at the Redway Tavern at **Langley**, the Eagle and Child at **Gradbach**, and the Setter Dog at **Walker Barn**.

Among **Buxton's** main coaching inns were the White Hart, in Scarsdale Place, and the Eagle, rebuilt by the 4th Duke of Devonshire in 1760. It was originally called the Eagle and Child, which like the former pub at Gradbach refers to the crest of the Earl of Derby (see Chapter 4).

As you would expect of a popular spa town like Buxton, a considerable number of pubs and hotels have come and gone, including the Seven Stars (later called the Dog and Partridge), Oddfellows Arms on the High Street, and the Swan-with-Two-Necks on Windsor Road. The Fox and Hounds was once to be found on West Road, the Horseshoe was located on Fairfield Road, and the Red Lion in Holmefield. The Shakespeare Inn on Spring Gardens was another coaching inn which in its time was very popular, but after its lease expired in 1926 it was knocked down to make way for shops.

In 1811 Buxton had 17 hotels and inns, including the Shoulder of Mutton which is first recorded in that year. It was here, in about 1850, that a soldier by the name of Dawson was found guilty of having a drink without paying for it. He was taken across the road, tied to a tree and flogged, much to the displeasure of the regulars who felt he had been hard done by. So they began to boycott the pub and went elsewhere, and in an effort to restore the image of his premises, the landlord decided to change the pub's name to the Swan.

At **Dove Holes** the Railway Inn closed in 1994 and is now a joinery supplier, while at **Chapel-en-le-Frith** the Pack Horse has been renamed the Royal Oak. However, the Bull's Head and Swan-with-Two-Necks have both vanished.

Incidentally, like its Buxton counterpart, the latter's name is almost certainly a corruption of the name A Swan with Two *Nicks*. This is derived from the annual 'swan-upping' procedure whereby the birds on special rivers such as the Thames were marked by their owners – five nicks in the case of a royal swan, and two if it was owned by the Dyers and Vintners Companies. At **Horwich End**, the Jolly Roger (also the New Inn for a bit) closed around 15 years ago and is now an antiques shop.

At **Chinley**, north of Chapel, the old Squirrel Inn was replaced by the much grander Princes Hotel to cater for the increased railway traffic, and this was later renamed the Chinley Lodge Hotel. Nearby, at **Whitehough**, was the historic Whitehough Old Hall, and for many years you could once enjoy a pint in the Red Cow Inn which stood next door (it closed about a century ago).

Former pubs at **Buxworth** include the Bull's Head Inn, which closed in 1960 and became a private residence (the house is now called the Old Bull's Head); and the Rose and Crown, which used to stand by the upper canal basin. When the canal's fortunes dipped in the early years of the twentieth century the pub became a farm, and was later demolished. It's reported that the stones from the building were used in the restoration of the canal basin.

The Royal Oak at **Taxal**, a hamlet in the Goyt Valley near Whaley Bridge, once boasted a royal hunting lodge which in 1829 became the Royal Oak. In later years it changed its name to The Chimes, but that in turn closed around 20 years ago. Further west, into Cheshire, Rainow and Bollington appear to be peaceful and mostly rural communities, but both once echoed to the sounds of industry – and pubs. It is reported that **Rainow** once had nine, and **Bollington** still boasts 19 pubs and clubs.

A mile to the north of Bollington is a small village with the delightful name of **Pott Shrigley**, but the demise of its pub early in the last century is evidence if needed of the dire consequences of over-imbibing on the Sabbath. The Lowther Arms was named after the Lord of the Manor, and by all accounts was a pleasant village inn. But one particular Sunday morning in 1922 as Lady Constance Lowther was emerging from church she detected alcohol on the breath of her groom, and in a fit of moral rage promptly closed the village pub for good. However, there is a far more indecent version of this story (preferred by most locals, it has to be said) that has Lady Constance catching her groom relieving himself against the wheels of her carriage.

In **Hayfield**, the Bridge Inn closed in 1923 and is now a doctor's surgery; the Commercial Inn, opposite the Railway Inn (now the Kinder Lodge) ceased trading in 1908; and the Junction Inn called time in 1935. In 1958, three local pubs locked up for good: the Wood Inn on New Mills Road, the Toll Bar Inn on Glossop Road, and further along in **Little Hayfield**, the Grapes Inn had called its last orders.

Heading down the Sett Valley to **New Mills**, the Old Crescent Inn on Market Street closed while this book was being written, and it is understood that the new owner intends to turn it into an Indian restaurant. A house called the Old Squirrel Inn on Buxton Road, near Newtown Station (New Mills), is another indication of an ex-pub. At the hamlet of **Rowarth** it is recorded that lost pubs included the Children's Inn and Moorfield Arms.

Heading eastwards to the central Peak once more, it is said that in the early 1800s **Eyam** boasted 11 pubs and as many as 23 ale houses. Former hostelries include the Town Head Inn, which opened as far back as the 1600s for passing packhorse teams and closed during the First World War. Moving down Church Street, the Royal Oak was originally called the British Oak and until it closed a few years ago, was a popular venue for local functions, with the Carnival Queen being crowned on the balcony at the front. The Rose and Crown used to occupy the building opposite the post office, while a little further along is the distinctive Brick House, where a seventeenth-century pub called the Stag's Parlour used to stand.

Opposite the church I remember once drinking in the Bull's Head (previously the Talbot, and before that the Shrewsbury Arms), but in the late 1990s it was sold off for redevelopment as private flats. At the eastern end of the village there were once two pubs on the Square: the Foresters Arms (now Foresters House) and the Bold Rodney, the latter dating from the late eighteenth century and named after Admiral Rodney, who trounced the French fleet in the Caribbean in 1782. It closed in 1901, and now forms part of the Eyam Tea Rooms, which in the evenings is transformed into the Bold Rodney Bistro.

The former pubs of Eyam have been well documented in an interesting booklet compiled by Eyam Village Society, available locally, and those which are now private buildings – like the Town Head Inn, Brick House and Bull's Head – have green heritage plaques attached to their exterior to denote their previous role.

Along the road at **Foolow** the Bull's Head was once joined by the Three Horse Shoes, long since demolished, and the Bird in Hand. The latter was renamed the Spread Eagle and closed in 1911, but the building survives.

At **Stoney Middleton** there have been as many as 15 pubs in the village over the last 200 years, but all that's left standing today is the Moon Inn (originally called the Old Moon and sited across the road). Other ex-pubs include the Bull's Head, Royal Oak, Miner's Arms, Grouse, Boot and Shoe, and Stag's Head – the last knocked down for road-widening. The Ball Inn used to stand at the junction of Eyam Dale and Stoney Middleton Dale, but this has been demolished and is now a car park for the quarry opposite.

One especially noteworthy pub was the Lovers Leap Inn, located almost under the rock of the same name and which is famous as being the scene of Hannah Baddeley's jump in 1762. According to the story, she threw herself off the top in a suicide bid, but was saved when her petticoat billowed out like a parachute and wafted her safely down.

Moving north to the Hope Valley, and one of the most unusual ex-pubs in the Peak District was to be found at **Castleton**, or more precisely in the gaping mouth of Peak Cavern (also known as the Devil's Arse and reputedly the largest cave entrance in Britain). Until the last century, the cave was used by rope-makers, since it offered the necessary space and ideal atmospheric conditions (ie damp). At the turn of

1800 it is recorded that the cavern's 60ft-high mouth supported several dwellings, including a beerhouse.

Bradwell's Newburgh Arms is now a now private house, while ex-pubs at **Hope** include the Blacksmith's Arms (at one time the Horse Shoe Inn) and the Durham Ox, which ended up becoming the village post office. The Cross Daggers Inn, now Daggers House, existed until 1860, and the sign for this attractive, 400-year-old building depicted crossed daggers, a posset pot, tankard and a bunch of grapes. Cross daggers represent the shield of the Cutlers' Company of Sheffield, and it is believed that salesmen carrying cutlery from Sheffield stayed here en route to Manchester.

Although the former Church Hotel at **Edale** was renamed the Rambler Inn, there was also once a Church Inn that is now Church Cottage. In the 1800s, **Grindleford** sported the Bluebell Inn on the main street; while in **Bamford** the former Cheshire Cheese Inn became the post office. I have also read that in the 1950s Dutton's Brewery demolished the 350-year-old Golden Fleece in Bamford, to considerable local protests, and replaced it with a pub called the Sir Winston Churchill nearby; but this too has evidently disappeared.

Hathersage has also seen its fair share of pubs coming and going. However, thanks to research by the Hathersage Millennium Group there is plenty of information about the changing fortunes of their locals. Following questionnaires and interviews with some of the older residents, the group established that the Buck Inn once stood alongside the 'Buck Stone', below the causeway under Stanage Edge. Gatehouse Farm used to be the Cowgate Inn; and Cliffe House on Jaggers Lane was once known as the Bull and Mouth (c1750).

The story goes that funeral processions would sometimes stop at the latter, as it was on the uphill route to the graveyard from next-door Bamford (which didn't have its own burial ground), and the coffin-bearers were sometimes in need of sustenance. High Lees Farm was the Hare and Hounds until 1917, located on the site of an earlier thatched inn; Hillfoot Farm on Castleton Road was the Hillfoot Inn, then the Rifleman's Arms until around 1880. Old Bell House in the village was formerly the Old Bell (or Blue Bell) Inn, while Hall Cottage was once frequented as the Angel and Child.

It is said that the Old Bell and Hare and Hounds both lost their licenses around the time of the First World War, when the authorities decided that there were too many pubs in the village. The Ordnance Arms Hotel on the Main Road was built in 1808 by Major A.

Shuttleworth, who had served in the Royal Artillery in the American War of Independence. In the 1960s it was renamed the Hathersage Inn, and only a few years ago closed down to become an outdoor equipment shop and residential flats.

Until around 1900 you could enjoy a drink in the Cross Daggers at **High Bradfield**, which because it was located near the gates of St Nicholas Church was locally known as 'Heaven's Parlour'. It was a popular haunt of the navvies who built the dams on the new reservoirs in the valley, so much so that it ended up losing its licence because they kept fighting all the time. The Cross Inn once stood in the centre of **Low Bradfield**, but closed in the late 1970s; while the George at **Dungworth** became a farmhouse after it closed in the 1950s.

Perhaps the most unusual – and crushingly final – end to a pub or hotel concerns the Ashopton Inn in the Upper Derwent Valley. It was built in 1824 as a halt for coaches on the Sheffield to Glossop turnpike, a chance to change horses, refresh and make preparations for the long haul over the Snake Pass, as well as a stopping point for weary travellers who had made it successfully the other way.

However, as already outlined in Chapter 6, the narrow valley was earmarked by the Derwent Valley Water Board to create the new Ladybower reservoir to meet the growing thirst of Sheffield and the East Midlands. Early in 1943, the villages of Derwent and **Ashopton**, including the Ashopton Inn and the equally elegant and historic Derwent Hall, were acquired so that building work on the massive new Ladybower dam could proceed. The water board did look into the possibility of rebuilding Ashopton Inn on a new site, but in the end the licence was transferred to premises at New Mills, and Ashopton and its ruined pub was permanently submerged beneath the water.

However, in the unusually dry summer of 1959, the water levels in the reservoirs dropped sufficiently for a local man to recover stones from the family farm he had been forced to give up 16 years before. He ended up using them as a rockery outside his new home in Ashbourne.

Smaller reservoirs dot the fringes of the Dark Peak, including **Redmires** on the north west edge of Sheffield. What looks like a memorial stone by the road near the water is in fact a stone from a pub called the Grouse and Trout which used to stand near here.

In **Old Glossop**, the Hare and Hounds, Ring o'Bells and the Greyhound have all disappeared, and the Quiet Shepherd Inn near **Tintwistle** is now a private house. At **Crowden**, by Torside Reservoir in the remote valley of Longdendale, the Commercial Inn was pulled down in the 1920s. A similar fate befell the George and Dragon, which for over 300 years stood at the nearby Holmfirth turning and was closed in 1961 because Manchester Corporation deemed it too near their reservoir.

A mile up that road (by Heyden Bridge) there once stood the Tollemarche Arms, and if you headed eastwards you came to the Angel Inn which until the 1920s stood in the village of **Woodhead** above the station next to the tunnel entrance. Pub, village and railway are all long gone. Nearing the top of the Woodhead Pass the former hamlet of **Saltersbrook** once included the Miller's Arms (closed in 1913), while at the summit the Plough and Harrow is also long gone.

The latter became known as Fiddlers Green, after a semi-blind violin-player that used to entertain guests in the remote pub. The story goes that one night, almost certainly after a glass too many, he wandered out on to the featureless moors and got lost, ending up down at Ronksley Water where he was found minus his fiddle. Luckily for him, shepherds came across both his violin and case some time later and managed to reunite the grateful musician with his instrument. After that the pub was known as Fiddlers Green in memory of the fortunate man.

In all, there were once six inns on the Woodhead Road across the Dark Peak, but most fell victim to the changing times that saw the

One of the last shepherds' gatherings at the now-demolished Miller's Arms at Saltersbrook, at the head of the Woodhead Pass.

(photo courtesy of the Peak District National Park Authority)

railway (at least for a while) replace the road as the main trans-Pennine transport route, and the water authorities exercising their political clout to safeguard their supplies. Today it's a bleak and rather soulless valley, and at the summit in particular there is virtually nothing, save a few forlorn stones amid the desolate moorland, to remind us of past pubs.

Finally, there are two other remote, moorland pubs with unusual names and both long consigned to the South Pennines history books. Bill o'Jacks was located near the reservoirs on the moors above **Greenfield**, and gained notoriety and national headlines in 1832 after the double murder of landlord William Bradbury and his son.

The Isle of Skye Inn, near **Holmfirth**, may have disappeared many years ago, but the pub is still remembered by the annual Four Inns challenge walk, in which pre-registered teams of four have to complete a gruelling 45-mile hillwalk in 24 hours. The route was devised in 1922 by the legendary Fred Heardman, one-time landlord of both the Old Nag's Head and Rambler Inn at Edale (see below).

In 1957, the 51st Derby Rover Scouts organised the first Four Inns race, which then as now begins at Holmbridge, on the southern edge of Holmfirth, and from the site of the Isle of Skye pub heads south across the windswept moors of Black Hill, Bleaklow and Kinder Scout, taking in the Snake Pass Inn and Old Nag's Head at Edale. The entire route is off-road, across high and often boggy moorland tracks where the weather can be unpredictable to say the least. Good map-reading and navigation skills are as important as fitness and stamina. The route continues via Chapel-en-le-Frith and the Goyt Valley to reach the last pub – the Cat and Fiddle – high on the Cheshire moors, after which the weary and footsore walkers stagger down the old Roman road to finish at Harpur Hill on the edge of Buxton.

To give some idea of the seriousness of the challenge, three Rover Scouts died from fatigue and hypothermia while attempting the Four Inns Walk in March 1964. But it was out of this tragedy that the Peak District Mountain Rescue service was born.

Figments of the imagination

In recent years the Peak District, like other attractive areas of England's northern hill country, such as the Yorkshire Dales and North York Moors, has provided the setting for numerous TV series and adaptations. The long-running comedy *Last of the Summer Wine* is set in and around Holmfirth on the northern (West Yorkshire) edge of the National Park, while the popular *Peak Practice* series about rural doctors was

A popular walkers' haunt, the Old Nag's Head at Edale marks the southern terminus of the Pennine Way, and is one of the stops on the Four Inns challenge walk.

filmed in the White Peak and variously centred on Ashover, Crich, Longnor and Wirksworth.

Quite often the setting switched from the doctor's surgery to the village pub, and this meant good business for the (genuine) local, which surrendered part or more usually all of its premises for the day. The Black Horse at Ashover featured in several programmes under its own name, but when the cameras rolled at Longnor, the Horseshoe Inn was temporarily renamed the Inn on the Square.

The village of Birchover, mid-way between Bakewell and Matlock, has also had its fair share of fictitious pubs. In 1986, Uppertown Farm featured in an ITV production of a Sherlock Holmes story called *The Mystery of Priory School*, when it was converted into a period pub called the Champion Jack, featuring a cockerel on the sign. According to Jim Drury's entertaining recollections on life in Birchover, the fee paid to the farmer allowed for substantial redecorations, and the timber left by the film crew was enough to repair every gate on the farm. Some years earlier, one of Birchover's two real pubs, the Druid Inn, was dressed up as an Irish tavern for a film which sadly was never shown.

In the small Staffordshire village of Alstonefield, a pub called the White Swan materialised during the filming of *The Life and Times of Henry Pratt*; while in the 1970s, passers-by at the hamlet of Gratton, between Youlgrave and Elton, were surprised to see a sign for the non-existent Black Dog inn. It was created solely for the filming of D.H. Lawrence's book *The Virgin and the Gypsy*.

More than just a pub

For me, one of the best things about visiting a new pub, especially if it's a freehouse (not owned by a brewery or pub chain) and if it has a little bit of history, is that apart from the beer you never quite know what you might find inside. By now, this book should have pointed you in the direction of a number of distinctive and characterful establishments, but others have equally unusual surprises in store.

For instance, there are pubs in the Peak District with wells actually inside the bar, such as the Mermaid Inn on the Staffordshire moors near Leek, and the Red Lion at Birchover. At the latter you can peer down the illuminated 30ft, glass-topped well and learn that it previously served as the building's water supply, as well as getting a little bit of a shock where you see a skull staring up at you from the bottom.

Meanwhile, beside the Hanging Gate pub, west of Chapel en le Frith, is the Cockyard Mission. It's a long, low hut, partly made of corrugated iron with a moss-covered roof and which stands in the middle of the pub car park. As odd as it may seem, this incongruous building is a consecrated chapel, part of the local diocese, and holds two services a month.

Some pubs have expanded into the entertainment business, but the clientele can vary in age and nature. The Knockerdown Inn, near Carsington Water, contains a growing menagerie of animals that attract a big family audience. The original seventeenth-century farm became a pub in the 1830s, and used to be called the Greyhound. Today young visitors, in particular, are attracted by the two- and four-footed residents who live in the fields out the back, including donkeys, chickens – and even ostriches.

A generally older audience tends to patronise the Fishpond Inn at Matlock Bath, a low-set, eighteenth-century pub where live music has helped this lively and popular venue continue to do well. Located opposite the Grand Pavilion, it's named after the stock pond across the road that is fed by the resort's famous thermal waters, and in which a seemingly contented shoal of fish appear to thrive.

The pub's grand, first-floor ballroom holds 230 and has a beautiful arched ceiling and a sprung dance floor, and is the venue for a variety of performances – everything from rock through to folk and dance. In addition, there are occasional illustrated lectures and talks, and Matlock Film Society has also begun to use it to show films. There are usually at least two gigs a week, plus a weekend session in the bar; and the pub even has its own CDs of groups and artists recorded live at the pub.

Live artistic performances are also the order of the day at the Old Poets Corner at Ashover. Formerly the Red Lion, this high, twin-gabled, mock-Tudor pub on Butts Road is now run by a couple who were previously in charge of the Dead Poets Inn at Holbrook. They stage regular music and poetry evenings, as well as placing a firm emphasis on the core values of the traditional public house.

Joint licensee Kim Beresford told the *Matlock Mercury*: "We wanted to create something different. Our philosophy is that a pub is for drinking, with people wanting to come for good ale and good conversation. We do everything ourselves, the food is home cooked, we are a free house, and we choose all the entertainment ourselves and not on recommendations from managers or agencies."

They even host their own beer festival, featuring dozens of real ales, ciders and fruit wines, and accompanied by live folk, jazz and blues sets. Indeed, the pub sign outside reads: 'Bread is the staff of life, but Beer is life itself…' Amen to that.

Rather different pub entertainment is staged at the Winking Man, high on the moors above Leek by the A53 Longnor turning. A self-styled country club and disco, it resembles an oversized transport cafe, decorated with rows of coloured lights and surrounded by a vast car park. There's dancing every Saturday evening at 'Winkers', plus regular karaoke and rock nights, and at around 1,150ft (350m) high it claims it is the highest nightclub above sea level in England.

Incidentally, the pub takes its name from an unusually-shaped rock up on nearby Ramshaw Rocks. When viewed from the A53 as you drive up from Leek, a hole in this particular rock looks like the profile of a head complete with an eye. If you keep looking as you drive past, the effect of the rocks behind suddenly blocking the light seems to cause the eye to wink.

The contrast between the Winking Man and the no-frills Royal Cottage, a throwback to a traditional rural beerhouse and located within sight just 100 metres up the road, couldn't be much greater. (See Chapter 2 for more on the Royal Cottage.) And all this high up on the high and windy Staffordshire moorland.

Another example of how some rural pubs in the Peak District have branched out is that, in addition to your summer afternoon pint, you can also book a helicopter ride from the next door field. It's a seasonal activity, of course, limited to a certain number of rides from specific pubs, including the Cat and Fiddle, the Moorland at Owler Bar, and the Grouse at Chunal, south of Glossop.

It has to be said that it's not to everyone's taste, since the sound of a clattering helicopter whizzing from pub to pub is hardly conducive to a peaceful day out in the countryside. But if you thought that some pub car parks were getting big then just wait until you see the first helicopter pad.

Elsewhere, publicans in the Peak District have been using their ingenuity in order to maintain the pub as a focal point of local community life, while at the same time broadening their appeal. Mirroring developments in a few other rural locations, several Peak pubs have diversified by welcoming new and entirely different strands of business. In addition to the usual pub noticeboard, you can now find a Post Office sign on the outside of one or two premises.

When the village shop and post office closed at Earl Sterndale the pub stepped in, and now every Wednesday and Friday afternoon you can buy your stamps and weigh your parcels in the Games Room of the Quiet Woman. A similar thing has happened at the Barley Mow at Kirk Ireton, where the post office now operates on a daily basis from an outbuilding of the pub called the Stable Shop.

The fact that pubs in the Peak District are prepared to diversify in this way is important on a number of counts. It offers real support for small and often quite remote rural communities where, as indicated above, the loss of the sole village shop or post office is nothing short of a death knell for the social fabric of the place. It also helps to bolster the position of the public house at the heart of the community – whether it's providing post office facilities or a meeting place for village groups and societies; and also it might just be a lifeline for the pubs themselves.

According to CAMRA, rural pubs across Britain have been closing at the rate of as many as 20 a month – a staggering figure – with the majority forced out by escalating property prices. You would think that pubs in most towns and villages of the Peak District, a busy National Park and popular holiday destination, would perhaps be less at risk than some other far-flung places of the country. But the list of ex-pubs outlined at the beginning of this chapter tells a different story, and while some will simply go out of business or close as a matter of course, it's surprising to find that even places on the mainstream tourist circuit don't necessarily seem to be able to support more than one pub.

Take Eyam, for instance, an ostensibly thriving community and a popular destination for coachloads of visitors throughout the year who come to learn about the historic plague village. As recently as 25 years ago there were four pubs to choose from, but one after the other – the Rose and Crown, Royal Oak and Bull's Head – have all been sold off for conversion to private houses. Now only the Miner's Arms is left to service a large, busy village in the heart of the Peak District.

However, some village locals have been fighting back, encouraged by an initiative launched in 2001 called 'The Pub is the Hub'. The scheme is jointly run by the Countryside Agency and the British Beer and Pub Association, and helps local communities as well as breweries and individual landlords use their entrepreneurial skills to come up with ideas to strengthen the role and function of the traditional village pub.

Diversification is the key, which is why the post office facilities at the Quiet Woman and the Barley Mow have been replicated at a number of other pubs across the country. In fact, this has already gone a stage further, and there are now village pubs in deepest England which variously host a bookshop, bookmakers, and arts and crafts shop. A few years ago, Derby University hired out a room above the Miner's Arms in the Peak District village of Brassington and held computer classes for local people, and further initiatives will hopefully follow.

Home brew

Other landlords are inventive in a more traditional way, and one of the most enterprising is David Allingham at the Bentley Brook Inn. This imposing, half-timbered hotel sits on the A515 just to the north of Ashbourne at Fenny Bentley, but the establishment is about far more than just bed and breakfast.

The Bentley Brook Inn is the home of Leatherbritches Brewery, founded in 1995, and whose name is a throwback to the Middle Ages when officials known as ale conners would go around checking the strength and suitability of new brews. Other than tasting it, a common method was to pour a little of the beer on a bench and sit in it for a while – if the ale conner's breeches were semi-stuck to the bench then the brew was of a satisfactory strength. Not surprisingly an ale conner's outfit came to include a pair of leather breeches.

The Bentley Brook Inn at Fenny Bentley is a splendid period house standing in eight acres of grounds.

The Bentley Brook Inn is home to Leatherbritches Brewery, as well as having its own kitchen garden and nursery.

This painting by Cherry Burns-Salmond depicts the so-called ale conners at work outside Leatherbritches Brewery. The image is emblazoned on the pub's own mugs.

Leatherbritches produces a small range of traditional cask conditioned bottled beers, including the ever-popular Hairy Helmet and one or two specialist brews, such as a porter. Production takes place in a small outbuilding to the rear of the pub – Burton-on-Trent this isn't – and viewing can be arranged by prior arrangement ('viewing' because it's too small for tours, they say).

David Allingham lovingly describes the scene: "When the wart and hops are boiling it is worth being in the brewery yard just for the aroma that floats from the chimney. Truly, it is a fragrance more comforting than newly-baked bread or even early morning bacon."

If you don't fancy sampling the end result in the bar, you can always take a bottle or two home for future enjoyment. In addition to the brewing, the Bentley Brook Inn also hosts occasional beer festivals, when real ale lovers descend on a marquee out the front of the pub which is crammed with barrels from breweries around the country.

As well as brewing, the ten-bedroomed hotel, which until 1956 was a private residence, also produces home-made fine foods, including jams and pickles, biscuits and fudges, as well as tasty sausages. Across the road is the Leatherbritches Kitchen Garden and Nursery, where for two centuries fruit, vegetables and herbs have been grown for the table of the house – and now for patrons of the hotel, as well as to take away. All the plants are grown from English seed, plugs or cuttings.

Another brewing pub is located at Marsden in West Yorkshire, on the extreme northern edge of the Peak District. Here, in the same year that Leatherbritches was founded, the Riverhead Brewery Tap opened inside a carefully renovated, three storey grocers' shop on Peel Street, and you can actually view the full mash brewery through an observation window at the back of the bar.

Each beer is named after local reservoirs, the higher their altitude the higher the respective gravity of the beer: Sparth Mild, Butterley Bitter, Deer Hill Porter, Cupwith Light Bitter, Black Moss Stout, March Haigh Special Bitter and Redbrook Premium Bitter. Another speciality to look out for is Ruby Tuesday, which is a strong pink cider made in Yorkshire. The Riverhead Brewery Tap won the CAMRA Pub of the Year award in 2001, and has scooped the Summer Pub of the Year accolade several times.

Small-scale brewing also takes place near Hartington, where Whim has produced good quality ales since 1993 which are available in selected pubs in Derbyshire and Staffordshire. Sheffield brewers Kelham Island have also begun brewing at Thornbridge Hall, near

Ashford in the Water (it's called the Thornbridge Hall Country Brewery); while a new micro-brewery has been established on the Chatsworth estate in a converted barn between Baslow and Edensor (known as the Barn Brewery producing Peak Ales including the well-received Bakewell Bitter).

Another new enterprise is the Edale Brewing Company, begun in 2001 by lawyer-turned-brewer Richard Grimes, and which produces such evocatively named beers as Ringing Roger, Kinder Stout and Kinder Trespass. Still a relatively small-scale operation, it supplies a few local pubs, including the Cheshire Cheese in Hope, the Navigation at Buxworth and the Monsal Head Hotel; and in 2004 the new company purchased the Hillsborough Hotel in Sheffield from where they hope to brew in larger quantities.

Changing times

As social and recreational trends develop, it's inevitable that this will be reflected in the changing nature and distribution of pubs and inns. We've already seen how the temperance movement sought to cut the sheer number of alehouses and pubs, and quite successfully too; and how pressures and challenges from a variety of directions have pushed some of the less efficient or well-managed public houses under.

In the last few decades, our growing affluence and leisure time have meant that more and more Peak pubs have begun to specialise in high-quality meals, and if some establishments appear little more than rural restaurants, then that's simply a reflection of changing patterns in recreation and socialising.

The Rambler Inn at Edale is a good example. This large Victorian house, built early in the twentieth century, was for many years known as the Church Hotel, then later the Jolly Rambler, as weekend crowds alighted from the Sheffield and Manchester trains to enjoy a day's walking in the hills.

The Old Nag's Head just up the road, located at the start of the Pennine Way, is equally busy over a summer's weekend, although today there will probably be as many car-bound visitors as those pulling on walking boots.

In the 1930s, the Cyclists' Touring Club had over 4,000 inns on their books, all of which carried the club sign and offered bed and breakfast. Today there are guides to pubs that cover all manner of things: those that serve proper real ale, or have facilities for children and families; the ones that have an absence of piped music or jukeboxes, or others that specifically welcome dogs; and of course pubs who have specialist menus.

Today the Rambler Inn at Edale styles itself a 'Country House Hotel', with its rooms named after the various 'booths' (old shepherd's huts) around Edale. It even hosts a so-called 'folk train' where musicians and beer drinkers join forces for an organised trip along the scenic Hope Valley line and back.

Another traditional rural pub given the modern treatment is the Stanhope Arms at Dunford Bridge. Already alluded to in previous chapters, this nineteenth-century former shooting lodge in the middle of the South Yorkshire moors south of Holmfirth was built by the Stanhope family who used it for just a few weeks 'recreation' each year. In 1947 it was bought by the Barnsley Brewing Company and turned into a pub.

Its high-ceilinged rooms and ornate fireplaces exuded a period elegance, and there was even a snug bar of sorts to the rear of the main bar. However, a new owner recently stepped in and after a complete facelift in 2003 re-opened 'The Stanhope' as an entirely different concern. "It's elegant, chic, modern, bright, airy and minimalist in style," according to the description on the pub's website.

The snug bar has given way to extra kitchen space, and the lounge now boasts black leather sofas and trendy furniture. In the open-plan restaurant the deliberately plain white walls feature a silver dado rail where wall vases each hold a single lily, and all this contributes to what they describe as "a truly contemporary dining experience". It's light, airy and extremely stylish, and by all accounts the jazz suppers are a real hoot; but when does a pub stop being a pub?

The emergence of so-called roadhouse pubs in the mid twentieth century signalled a change in the nature of many rural pubs in places like the Peak District, and it has been exacerbated by the emergence of national pub and hotel chains which continue to buy up the more prominent or profitable establishments.

But even the town centres of the Peak are not exempt when it comes to the changing face of the modern public house. Bakewell boasts the popular Australian Bar; Ashbourne has its Johnson's Bar, most appropriately given that it's part of the Green Man Hotel; and with the University of Derby opening a campus at Buxton, there's every likelihood that the pubs and clubs of that rather genteel old spa town will receive a shot in the arm.

Already the chain J.D. Wetherspoon has re-opened the former

Midland Hotel (built in the 1870s) as Wye Bridge House (which was its original name). In Matlock, it also runs the Crown in the town centre, which was previously a shop.

Around the fringes of the Peak, in particular, there are a number of large, old pubs which have been given the branded treatment. Examples include the Peacock (Chef and Brewer) at Owler Bar, where you can also find the Moorland run by Brewsters (which also has the Highwayman at Eastmoor); while the Fox House Inn and Ram's Head at Disley are both owned by Vintage Inns.

Everything, inevitably, is standardised – from the interior décor to the menus and even the style of the actual pub signs – which on the one hand is fine if you want an unchallenging and reassuringly familiar place to go, but on the other is largely devoid of any distinctiveness, save the shape of the building or the view out of the window. Mind you, at least these places are still pubs, rather than turned into luxury apartments or holiday flats.

However, after chronicling all the pubs which have closed or have become irredeemably altered, how better to finish than by profiling a modern village pub which virtually rose from the ashes?

The peaceful village of Sheldon, two miles west of Bakewell, seems very similar to all the other traditional limestone villages of the White Peak, and at first glance the solid and unshowy, stone-built pub seems to have been around since the time of the miners who once worked nearby Magpie Mine for lead (see Chapter 3).

But remarkably the Cock and Pullet is little more than ten years old, and was originally a barn which stood next door to the former village pub, the Devonshire Arms, which closed in 1971. The barn once held village dances, and its conversion was quite a challenge for its owners and Sheldon residents David and Kath Melland.

"It was quite a gamble in this day and age when village pubs are closing," admits Kath, "but we had a lot of encouragement from the village." Despite the need for endless form-filling, the Peak District National Park authority was also supportive, but of course it helped enormously that David Melland was a builder by trade. Mind you, there was little of the original building left – nothing at the back, no windows at the front, and a cellar that had to be dug from scratch. It took around 18 months to complete, and opened in August 1995.

The Cock and Pullet stands half way up Sheldon's wide main street, its modest exterior disguising the fact that inside it's been converted with care and style. There's full disabled access, a sheltered patio to the rear, and three en-suite bedrooms upstairs. The dark and cosy bar is illuminated by a glowing open fire, and there's a separate no-smoking eating area. And, at virtually every quarter hour, a chiming sound somewhere or other in the bar will alert you to the fact that the landlord has on display his collection of 22 clocks.

More than anything else, the Cock and Pullet has once again provided a focal point for a fairly isolated village too small for any shops or other services. "We get all-comers," says Kath, "locals as well as visitors. We're open all day every day, with no strict rules or regulations, so that we welcome walkers and car drivers, with well-behaved children and dogs."

But local people also use the pub, and despite the presence of the nearby public hall, some village meetings are held in the pub, especially in the winter when the warming fire proves quite a lure. Local gamekeepers meet and dine at the Cock and Pullet, and the pub also has two pool teams and two darts teams.

Building your own pub might have been hard work, says Kath Melland, but running it is certainly a full-time business. "You have to work hard at it, but you also have to love it – it's a way of life, really."

The pub, it seems, can still be at the heart of village life in the Peak District.